# Iota

**By the same author**

Novels
*The River Running by*
*The Raging of the Sea*
*The Believer*
*Armada*
*The Fighting Spirit*
*The Crying of the Wind*
*Jannaway's Mutiny*

Philosophy
*Basic Flying Instruction*

Memoir
*A Good Boy Tomorrow*

Travel
*Seven stories from Blackwood's Magazine*

# IOTA
## God as Nature, Nature as God

*Charles Gidley Wheeler*

**Iota, God as Nature, Nature as God**

© 2008 Charles Gidley Wheeler

This book is print-on-demand and may be ordered through book stores, downloaded as an e-book, or ordered on the internet.

ISBN: 978-0-9559802-0-6

*We have seen that he who acts rightly from the true knowledge and love of right acts with freedom and constancy, whereas he who acts from fear of evil is under the constraint of evil and acts in bondage and external control.*

Baruch Spinoza

# Infinite

Something exists
Something infinite
Infinitely infinite

Infinite energy
Infinite matter
Infinite space
Infinite time
Infinite intellect

No beginning
No end
Its own cause
Self-created
Self-energized
Self-conceived
Self-perpetuated

From this Infinite no being can be excluded
No thing of any sort can stand apart

The Infinite I is in every thing
Everything is in the infinite I
Every thing is a finite mode
An iota within Iota

That fine cobweb outside the window
The diving swallows
This wheelchair
All memories
All experience
All science
All philosophy
All faith

Charles Darwin
Billy Graham
Adolph Hitler
Mother Teresa,
Osama Bin Laden
George W. Bush
The Dalai Lama
Mao Tse-tung

The dragonfly and the nuclear missile
The shotgun and the pheasant
The palace and the hovel
The proud and the penitent

All are finite modes
Temporary ways of being
Expressions of the infinite I
Parts of the eternal Self

You, She, Him, They
We share one identity
We are temporary eddies in a river
An infinitely deep river
A river with no banks

**One**

Everything is in every thing
Every thing is in everything

The Infinite is one and eternal
Nothing can stand outside this One
There is no outside
No absolute
Only the infinite and eternal I
The I that is indivisible

It is One
The One that is cause of itself

Events are one
We are events
Every event is determined by the One
The One is determined by every event
Events are effects of causes and causes of effects
Cause *is* effect and effect *is* cause
*We* are causes and effects
There is no separating us
We are One

Though we think we are free we are not free
Only the One, the infinite and eternal I is free

There can be no absolutes in the One
No absolute time
No absolute space
No absolute simultaneity
No absolute beginning
No absolute end
No absolute god
No absolute entities

No entity can be absolutely separate from another
For an absolute entity to exist it could not touch or blend with anything
It would have to be a one separated from the One
It would have to be separated by a gap
A gap of nothingness
A gap of nothing
Nothing at all
No magnetic field
No energy
No gravity
No nuclear force

Not even the whisper of the faintest cosmic breeze
Or the unheard buzz and whirr of quanta

For an entity other than the infinite One to exist
It would have to be separated by nothing
Nothing at all
So –
It would not be separate
It would not be an entity

The infinite One is 'full up'
It is a plenum
Bound together by the infinite power of conatus
The all inclusive force
The force of forces

Every living thing is joined to every other living thing
Every thought to every other thought
Every human to every virus
Every hyena to every butterfly
Every ant to every anteater

The silk worm in its cocoon
The pilot in his bomber
The robin in its nest
The prisoner on death row
The cockroach in the kitchen
The admiral on his bridge
The murderer and the murdered
The abuser and the abused
The conqueror and the conquered

Pope
President
Priest
Prime minister
Prima Donna

You
Me
Us
Them

We are part of the infinite and eternal One

**Two**

We are dualistic animals
We think in two's
This is the way we are

Left, right
Up, down
High, low
Fast, slow
Big, small
Hot, cold

Mind, matter
Concept, object
Knowledge, ignorance
Justice, injustice
Good, evil
Health, sickness

Day, night
Beginning, end
Birth, death
Pleasure, pain
Reason, unreason
Truth, falsehood
Light, darkness
Artisan, artefact

Through such dualities we conceive reality
But they are not separate or separated
They are aspects of the Infinite One

## Aspects

Our intellect is limited to two aspects
Each aspect forms one side of an equation
Each equation is an expression of identity
A way of referring
An aspect of reality

Thought, matter
*Noumenon, phenomenon*
Will, representation
Software, hardware
A script, its enactment
A musical score, its performance
Wave, particle

Mind = Body
$E = mc^2$
God = Nature

But –

The infinite One
The self-causing, self-energizing
Unlimited and eternal One
Conceives itself
Perfectly and simultaneously
Under infinite aspects

And this
*is*

# IOTA

*Absolute.* The property of standing on its own, separate from all else.

*God.* A supernatural, omniscient, omnipotent being, believed to exist in an absolute relationship to the universe and the human species.

*Iota.* Reality, or all that is, from which nothing that has being or existence is, or can be, excluded.

*Unity of existence.* If we believe that God exists, we cannot consistently believe that God is not part of existence. If we believe that we exist, we cannot consistently believe that we are not part of that same existence. So if we believe that God exists and we exist, we have to accept that we and God are united and that we belong to and are part of the same single existence.

*The infinite.* If we speak of God as 'the Infinite Being', we cannot do so by half measures. Any property that we attribute to a truly infinite being must itself be infinite. If we speak of such a being with regard to time, we can only do so in terms of infinite time, or eternity. If we speak of it with regard to intelligence, we can only do so in terms of infinite intelligence. If we speak of it as extended, we can only speak of it in terms of infinite extension. Any property we attribute to the infinite being must necessarily be attributed infinitely.

*Three properties attributed to God.* Most theists will agree that the infinite God they worship or believe in is omnipotent, omniscient and omnipresent. But holding such beliefs rules out the possibility of belief in a god who stands in an absolute relation to the universe – for the following reasons:

*Omnipotence.* If we claim that God is infinitely powerful, we have to admit that wherever power (or energy) exists it is of God, and that there is no power (or energy) at all apart from God's power.

*Omniscience.* If we claim that God is infinitely intelligent, we have to admit that wherever intelligence exists it is of God, and that there is no intelligence apart from God's intelligence.

*Omnipresence.* If we believe that God is infinitely present, we have to admit that nothing exists in the physical world where God is not present.

*No exceptions to these conditional inferences.* We can make no exceptions to the above three conditionals, nor can we moderate them in any way. We have to believe that God's power and intelligence is in every molecule, quark, neutron and electron. We have to believe that every stone, every tree, every human being and every animal is God through and through, both as regards power, intellect and will.

*Indivisibility of intelligence.* If we believe in God's omnipresence and infinite intelligence, we cannot deny that intelligence also pervades the physical world. Each living being uses intelligence in the way its physical body permits. Examples of animal intelligence – in apes, elephants, porpoises and orangutans – abound. Just because we cannot carry on a conversation with a giraffe does not mean to say that a giraffe has no intelligence.

*Indivisibility of will.* If we believe in the indivisibility of intelligence, we have to accept that volition, or will, is also indivisible. On that basis, we have to abandon belief in individual free will.

*Identity of God with Nature.* Once it has been accepted that God is indivisible, omnipotent, omniscient and omnipresent there can be no difficulty in comprehending that wherever there is God there is Nature, and wherever there is Nature there is God. 'They' are one. That one is Iota.

*God, Nature and Iota.* Use of the word 'God' induces us to think in theistic terms of a creator who stands in an absolute relation to, and is external to, 'his' creation. Because we identify God with Nature, we could legitimately substitute the word 'Nature' for 'God' wherever 'God' appears in the text of this treatise. But this would be equally confusing, and that is why we have coined the acronymic name 'Iota', which contains within itself the concept of an Infinite, self-causing One which we humans conceive under the Two Aspects of thought and matter (or extension).

*An analogy to the Spinozan view.* If I had a perfect understanding of a computer program, my mind would conceive of it in terms of non-material language, or 'software'. If the language of the software were to be recorded on a compact disc, it would be fully expressed in the physical matter of the electro-magnetically modified disc. The program would be conceivable, simultaneously and completely, under the aspect of software (or mind) and under the aspect of hardware (or matter), the one being the program's conception, the other its expression. We might say that the conception was the fact of the matter, and the expression was the matter of the fact. Now suppose this computer program to be infinite and self-causing, and simultaneously and completely expressed both by its hardware (matter) and its software (mind). Being infinite, nothing can stand outside it. This is what Spinoza calls *Deus-sive-Natura*, God-or-Nature, and what we now know as Iota.

*Indivisibility and unity.* That which is divided by one is undivided. When we count, we say: 'one, two, three, four, five, six, seven...' we do not say 'one over one, two over one, three over one, four over one, five over one, six over one, seven over one...' There is no need to say that, because we take it for granted that one goes into, or abides in, each number that number of times. In a similar way, when we refer to objects – earth, moon, Mary, crocodile – we do not say 'earth over one, moon over one, Mary over one, crocodile over one'. We take it for granted that one abides in every thing.

That one is Iota, the infinitely infinite, all-inclusive reality.

*God, Allah and Jehovah.* Christians, Muslims and Jews are united in their belief in a single God who stands in an absolute relation to his creation. But they are divided because they worship that God in different ways and under different names. Each name has its own historical and cultural connotations which divide it off from the other two, as do behavior, language, dress, diet and art.

*The smallest change for the greatest effect.* In the course of a discussion on how an ill-governed state might be most effectively improved, Socrates asked what smallest change would have the greatest effect. The same principle can be usefully applied to the problem of division within and between nations and cultures. By replacing the names 'God', 'Allah' and

'Jehovah' with a single name – Iota – we might, perhaps, make some headway in breaking down barriers between cultures and religions.

*Religion divides; absolutist religion divides absolutely.* While the members of absolutist religions are united in their belief in God, their leaders use that same belief as authority for claiming that theirs is the one true faith, and for separating themselves from the rest of the world population – including those who also believe that *theirs* is the one true faith, and that *theirs* is the one true doctrine. By taking up this stance they exhibit belief in a divisive God who prefers one religion to another.

*Humanism and absolutist religion.* Humanism puts humans first; religion puts religion first. Humanism is egalitarian; religion is hierarchical. Humanism is pacifist; religion is militant. Humanism is concerned with natural love for one's fellow human beings; religion is concerned with submission to the dictates of religious leaders who claim to be able to speak on behalf of God.

All that is good and useful about absolutist religions – and there is much good – stems not from religious doctrine, but from our common humanity. Religion is not the cause of our love for each other, or of noble or altruistic acts. The will to put the well-being of others before our own stems from no religious ordinance or divine command, but from our shared knowledge that we are united by our common humanity. Everything that is good about absolutist religions comes from this common knowledge; everything that is bad stems from its denial.

*Unity and division.* The human species is united by love, courage, kindness, generosity, magnanimity and self-sacrifice. It is divided by hatred, cowardice, revenge, envy, greed, pettiness and disregard for the well-being of others.

*The authority of religion.* Formalized religions are founded upon the ambition and will to power of those (usually men) who seek to take advantage of the willingness of gullible or disempowered people (usually women and children) to believe what they are told by those whose judgment, authority or scholarship they have been induced from their earliest years to respect.

*Religio-political correctness.* Even when the most erudite and scholarly academic, scientist or religious leader introduces a theory or preaches a sermon, we should never entirely let go our hold on the ability to reason sceptically. Down the centuries political leaders have used a combination of the sacred and profane – theology and science – as a way of persuading people to believe doctrines which, when examined by common sense, turn out to be absurd. Bishop Paley's 'argument from design' (which he purloined from Hume's character Cleanthes in *Dialogues Concerning Natural Religion*) is a good example of this practice. For nearly a century, the Paley's Watch analogy was compulsory reading for undergraduates at Cambridge University – a fine example of gullibility and religio-political correctness on the part of university professors as well as their students.

*Paley's Watch.* The argument superficially supports polytheism as well as monotheism: if I look at the ocean, why do I have to infer that it was created by the same god as the god who created trees, or the god who created bumble bees? After all, one man does not manufacture a watch, or a house – or for that matter a weapon of mass destruction.

*Gidley Wheeler's Machine Gun.* In crossing a heath, suppose I pitched my foot against a stone and were asked how the stone came to be there, I would probably answer that its existence was caused by an infinite causal chain of events. Nor would it be very easy to show that my answer was absurd. But suppose I found a machine gun upon the ground, and I were to be confronted with the question how the machine gun happened to be in that place. To be consistent, I could only give exactly the same answer, namely that the existence of the machine gun was brought about by an infinite causal chain; nor is there any reason why this answer should not serve for the machine gun as well as for the stone: it is equally admissible in the second case as in the first. When we inspect the machine gun, we find that its several parts are framed and put together for a specific purpose, e.g., that they are so formed and adjusted as to produce the projection of bullets at a very high velocity and in quick succession. The machine gun's mechanism being observed – it requires indeed, an examination of the weapon and perhaps some previous knowledge of the subject to perceive and understand it; but being once, as we have said, observed and understood, the inference we think is inevitable that the machine gun must have had a maker – that there must exist or have existed, at some time and at some place or other, an artificer or artificers who formed it for the purpose which we find it actually to answer, who comprehended its construction and designed it for the specific purpose of harming or killing living creatures, or otherwise doing damage to Nature. In the course of time, we would inevitably discover that the artificer or artificers who designed and manufactured the machine gun were human beings. To be consistent, we should then have to ask how those artificers came into existence. We could only answer by affirming, once again, that they came into being as a result of an infinite causal chain. If we were to answer that the artificers were brought into existence by another artificer, who, when he created them, knew very well what murderous weapons they would be capable of inventing, to be consistent in our method of enquiry we would then have to ask how the creating artificer came into being, and so *ad infinitum.* We are therefore driven to the conclusion that the infinite causal chain is Nature itself, and that Nature must necessarily be infinite, its own cause, and eternal – and that the supposition of an artificer, maker or creator who stands outside Nature is self-contradictory and absurd.

*The hierarchy of war.* Behind the soldier who kicks the door in and throws a grenade stands the sergeant. Behind the sergeant stands the platoon commander; behind the platoon commander stands the company commander; behind the company commander stands the battalion commander; behind the battalion commander stands the commander-in-chief; behind the commander-in-chief stands the head of state; behind the head of state stand religious leaders – and behind those religious leaders stand centuries of tradition, scholarship and fearsome authoritarian pronouncements concerning the afterlife, heaven and hell. For a soldier to stand up to such a huge weight of authority takes far more courage than is required to put on body amour and fire rockets at human beings whose faces he cannot see and whose families' grief he will never witness.

*Lambs to the slaughter.* Whether they are enlisted or civilian, and to whatever nation or religion they owe allegiance, those who are killed as a result of armed conflict do not willingly give their lives, nor do they make any sacrifice. They *are* the sacrifice, and their lives are taken from them by those people in power who believe – who *still* believe – that violence, war or terrorism can be of any benefit whatsoever to the human race.

*The stench of death.* All three absolutist religions subscribe to the commandment 'thou shalt not kill', and yet the leaders of all three religions condone war and killing, whether it is the rabbi's support for the Israeli tank commander who fires into Palestine, the Baptist pastor's support for the US submarine commander who fires a missile at Baghdad, or the imam's support for the terrorist who runs into a queue of university students and blows himself up. Such acts are only made possible by appeal to faith in an absolute God. Take that supposed God away, replace it with Iota and the knowledge that we are all one, and the thought of killing other human beings becomes repulsive – a metaphorical stench in our nostrils far more offensive than the stench of rotting flesh in hot sunshine.

*Faith, trust and epistemic authority.* Fear of punishment in a supposed after-life and belief in the immortality of the soul lie at the root of all religious faith. Such faith is not in God, but in the epistemic authority of human beings who claim to know God's will – including those who claim to have heard the voice of God. In order to have faith, it is first necessary to accept, trust and become subservient to another human being, whether a Jewish rabbi, a Christian priest, a Moslem imam or an evangelical preacher. Such people rely on rhetoric, book learning, mysticism and academic honors to set themselves above others. They use arguments of persuasion to persuade children, the oppressed, the bereaved, the mentally distressed, the lazy-minded and the gullible to adopt beliefs that are at best contradictory and at worst an insult to common sense.

And they are never called to account for the misery they cause or the conflict their teachings generate.

*The bungee jump and the leap of faith.* When you jump off a bridge on the end of an elastic rope, you do so in the firm belief that you will survive the experience – not because you believe God will keep you safe, but because you have faith in the manufacturers of the rope and its attachments, and in the people who help you put on your harness and make sure the attachments are properly fastened. The jump lasts only a matter of seconds, and, by and large, the attachments remain secure, the rope does not break and you do not die. On the other hand, when you attach yourself to an absolutist religion and make a leap of faith, you put your faith not in things that can be seen and tested or in a person who is accountable for your safety, but in people who are never held to account – people who persuade you to believe stories, myths and legends that were written down hundreds of years ago, are of doubtful authenticity and subject to wildly differing interpretations. In this case, however, the leap does not last for seconds but for a lifetime, and during that lifetime you will never know whether your belief in what people have told you (or what you have been encouraged to read) is true. Nor can the people who induced you to make that leap be held to account for any sense of failure or unhappiness that might accrue for yourself or your loved ones as a result of your adoption of the particular religious life to which you are committed. In some cases you may even be persuaded by a religious pedagogue to believe that if you strap a bomb to yourself and explode it in a busy market place in order to kill those who hold beliefs other than yours, you will secure yourself a place in paradise. Or, perhaps, you will be reassured that the war in which you or your next of kin is engaged is in an honorable cause for which it is worth dying.

While it is common for military leaders to suffer remorse and pangs of conscience about the people who have died in battle under their command, religious leaders suffer no such remorse with regard to the wrecked lives of those who believed their doctrines and obeyed their ordinances.

*Holy orders.* Why do people set themselves up as religious leaders? Answer: always vanity, always the will to power and sometimes, because they are human and have feelings of human love, the wish to 'do good'. No one with any genuine humility could ever mount a pulpit, wear vestments or publicly address God in prayer.

*Theological absolutism.* There is a logical contradiction implicit in belief in an absolute god who pre-exists Nature and is said to stand apart from and in an absolute relationship to Nature. Absolutist religions share the doctrine that the universe was created by an infinite Being that pre-existed a created universe; and that Being is said to have existed from all eternity. As such it is believed to be its own cause. This doctrine would be all very well were it not for the fact that we are also invited to believe that the supposed God and creation are entirely separate one from another, and stand in an absolute relationship to one another. If that were the case, God would have one sort of existence before the act of creation, and an entirely different sort of existence after it. But existence cannot be partitioned off in this way. This contradiction lies at the heart of many of the problems of philosophy and science and is *the* problem of theology.

*Incompatibility of monism with absolutism.* Belief that mind and matter, or soul and body, or God and Nature, are separate from one another presupposes absolutism and the belief that things are finite. Monism – the belief that mind and matter, or soul and body, or God and Nature are one – prohibits absolutism and necessitates belief in a single, infinite substance.

*Maths, mysticism and heresy.* Pythagoras was founder of a religious cult whose doctrine included belief in the transmigration and reincarnation of souls. He was also a mathematician. One of his disciples, Hippasos of Metapontum, is attributed with the discovery, in the 6th Century BCE, of the existence of irrational numbers – in particular that the square-root of 2 is irrational. At the time of his discovery, it was a tenet of religious faith among Pythagoreans that all numbers were rational, which is to say they could be expressed as whole numbers or the ratio of whole numbers. For denying this mathematical tenet of faith, Hippasos was condemned as a heretic. Legend has it that he revealed his discovery at sea, and that his Pythagorean colleagues threw him overboard.

In 1600 Giordano Bruno, the Renaissance Italian thinker, was denounced to the Inquisition for advocating cosmic monism – the belief that God and Nature are one and the same. He was burnt at the stake as a heretic in Rome. A few decades later, Spinoza was cursed and anathematized by his synagogue for much the same reason.

*The defeat of atomism.* Democritus, a student of

Leucippus in the 5th century BCE, was the co-originator of the theory that all matter is made up of imperishable atoms – indivisible elements or units which exist in a void, or empty space. His claim remained virtually unchallenged until the 19th century when Faraday argued that Newton was mistaken in supposing that force acted in a straight line through empty space 'at a distance', speculating instead that atoms were nothing more than centers of force. Ironically enough, Faraday was led to this conclusion by his own religious belief: he refused to accept that there could be such a thing as a void, as to do so would be to deny the omnipotence and omnipresence of God. Faraday's work provided Einstein with his starting point for the formulation of new laws of motion that would hold good for speeds up to that of light.

*Rejection of dualism.* The courage of Hippasos, Bruno, Spinoza, Faraday and Einstein lies in the fact that they were prepared to question what other mathematicians, physicists, scientists and theologians either took for granted or did not have the courage to question. In particular, Einstein realized that the concepts of absolute points in space, absolute moments in time and absolute simultaneity of events had to be discarded, and with them mind-body dualism and the concept of an absolute deity.

*Zero, Infinity and Time.* While mathematics does not admit the possibility of expressing zero as plus or minus and denies the possibility of absolute zero, it *does* allow us to speak of plus or minus infinity. The implication of this is that plus infinity and minus infinity are to be regarded as two different mathematical concepts. Time is treated in a similar way. For the purposes of many mathematical calculations, time is treated as being linear, the future and the past being regarded as being separated by a 'present moment in time', rather in the same way that plus values and minus values are separated by zero. The absolutist view of time is naïve and misleading – but essential to belief in the myths of creation and last judgment.

*There is no beginning.* Because past, present and future are all one, there can be no absolute beginning or absolute end. It is as absurd to suppose that Iota 'had' a beginning as it would be to suppose that it 'will have' an end. Similarly, measurement of the age of the universe in billions of 'years' is nonsensical – impressive, but nonsensical. Space and time exist as concepts in the human mind. We are not *in* time or space: space and time are concepts that are in us.

*Conceptual impossibility of theism.* We can conceive of a goat with golden horns or a man a hundred feet tall. But it is a conceptual impossibility to think of a triangle having parallel sides or the color red tasting of salt. Similarly it is conceptually impossible to conceive of a being who exists but whose existence is separate from, or precedes, our own. The only conceptually possible god is a demiurge which exists as part of Nature, in the same way that angels, archangels, seraphim, cherubim, devils etc are believed to exist as part of God's creation. But conceptual possibility provides no foundation for belief. Just because we can conceive of a goat with golden horns does not mean that such an animal exists; just because we can conceive of an angel called Gabriel provides no reason for believing in the existence of such a being.

*Defying reason.* The claim that an infinite creator exists separate from a finite creation flies in the face of reason: necessarily, a truly infinite being, which is to say a being with infinite attributes, must be all-inclusive. Nothing can stand outside an infinite being. To believe in an infinite god-creator who is separate from 'his' creation is to believe in a contradiction.

*How religion stretches the imagination.* Just as the prisoners in Plato's cave loved to be entertained by the dancing shadows on the wall, so do people like to be entertained by moving images and a good speaker. They like to be made to feel superior and they like having their imagination stretched. This is how religion works. It stretches the imagination beyond the elastic limit, so that a return to reason becomes not only sinful but impossible. By chanting prayers, reciting litanies, singing hymns and repeating credos, a sense of identity, power, community and exclusivity is achieved. Strange smelling incense, tinkling bells and conjuring tricks ('miracles') assist in giving the impression that the faithful are specially privileged to be in touch with something supernatural and mysterious. From that sense of privilege they gain a sense of power. But it is only a sense of power. It is only an illusion, just as the shadows on the wall in Plato's cave were an illusion.

*Indoctrination of beliefs.* Religious beliefs are instilled and reinforced by ceremony and repetition. Drama, music, art, sculpture, architecture and dance all play their part in stimulating religious feelings of fear, admiration, sympathy, love, pity and humility in the minds of religious congregations, and are used to persuade people into believing that they are special, and set apart from those who do not share the same beliefs – the prime example of this practice being, of course, the Jewish claim to be God's chosen people.

*The origin of 'us and them'.* Conflict within and between religions is rooted in resentment as a result of family disagreements, jealousy of wealth and disputes over territory. Necessarily, members of a religion, sect or cult belong to it because they believe that its beliefs, customs and ordinances are correct and that those of other religions are wrong – and in some cases sinful or blasphemous. It is not possible to be a committed believer in one religion and regard the beliefs of another religion as entirely correct. Thus is the 'us and them' attitude generated and perpetuated.

*Disagreements between Christians, Jews and Muslims.* Christian belief that Jesus is the son of God is an abomination to Jews and Muslims, as is the custom of placing images of men and women in churches. The Roman Catholic practice of praying to the Virgin Mary and the saints is an abomination to Protestants, as is the claim that the Pontiff is the infallible earthly representative of God. Jews believe that they are God's chosen people, and that Israel is the Promised Land given to them by God. Some Christians believe this and some do not. All Muslims reject the claim; many look forward to a time when Israel will be wiped off the map.

Jews call non-Jews gentiles; Muslims call non-Moslems infidels, and Christians condemn those without religious faith as pagan or atheist. But, undeniably, they are all human, just like you and me.

*Isaac and Ishmael.* Muslims regard Ishmael as Abraham's elder son, born by his wife's servant Hagar. Though born of Hagar, Ishmael was credited as Sarah's son in accordance with Mesopotamian law. Both Jewish and Islamic traditions consider Ishmael as the ancestor of the Arab people, but Judaism has generally viewed Ishmael as wicked. Judaism maintains that Isaac rather than Ishmael was the true heir of Abraham. Islamic tradition favors Ishmael, giving him a larger and more significant role. The Qu'ran views him as a prophet. According to the interpretation of some early theologians Ishmael, not Isaac, was the son that Abraham was called on to sacrifice, and whom Abraham believed would be the leader of a great nation.

*Disagreements within Islam.* The disagreement between Sunnis and Shias dates back to the years following Mohammed's death. Sunni Muslims hold that Abu Bakr was Mohammed's rightful successor, while Shia Muslims believe that Mohammed ordained his cousin and son-in-law Ali (the father of his only two grandsons Hasan ibn Ali and Husayn ibn Ali) to be the next caliph, making Ali and his direct descendants Mohammed's successors. Sunnis follow the Rashidun ('rightly-guided caliphs'), the first four caliphs who ruled after the death of Mohammed (Abu Bakr, Umar, Uthman Ibn Affan, and Ali). Shias discount the legitimacy of the first three caliphs and believe that Ali is the most divinely inspired man after Mohammed and that he and his descendants by Mohammed's daughter Fatimah, the Shia imams, are the sole legitimate Islamic leaders.

Unlike Sunni, Shia believe that special spiritual qualities have been granted not only to the Prophet Mohammed but also to Ali and the other imams. They are held to be immaculate from sin, and to have the ability to understand and interpret the hidden inner meaning of the teachings of Islam. The imams are believed to be trustees who bear the light of Mohammed in much the same way that popes, cardinals and bishops of the Roman Catholic church are believed by Catholics to be the trustees and guardians of the 'one true faith'.

*The messianic myth.* Christians, Jews and Muslims all look forward to the advent or return of a messiah or savior. Jews believe in the coming of a Messiah. Christians look forward to the second coming of Jesus Christ, whom they believe to be the Messiah. Muslims, particularly Shia and Sufi, believe that the Mahdi will appear in the last days to bring about a perfect and just Islamic society.

*Ascension into heaven.* Christians, Jews and Muslims share belief in the possibility of a human being ascending to heaven. Christians believe that Jesus ascended to heaven; Jews believe that Elijah ascended to heaven in a chariot of fire, and Muslims believe that Mohammed likewise ascended to heaven. Roman Catholics believe that the Virgin Mary was assumed bodily into heaven.

*Disagreements within the Christian Church.* The divisions and schisms within the Christian Church are innumerable. Only a few need be mentioned: Catholics, Protestants, Russian Orthodox Church, Greek Orthodox Church, Anglicans, Methodists, Baptists, Seventh-day Adventists, Jehovah's Witnesses, Plymouth Brethren, Quakers, Mormons, Christian Scientists, Amish, Exclusive Brethren, Open Brethren, Church of Jesus Christ and the Latter-day Saints, Christian Scientists, etc etc.

The schisms, family break-ups, misery, wars, martyrdom, torture and suffering that have resulted – and still result – from disagreements between squabbling Christians defies description.

*The Iotic principle.* Iota is one, infinite, and conceived under infinite attributes. Individual beings are finite modes of Iota. No part of Iota exists independently. Human beings are able to conceive Iota only under the aspects of thought and matter. Only Iota is free. All actions, thoughts, events and decisions are determined by Iota. We are all one. To hurt others is to hurt our collective self.

*The Iotic attitude.* We adopt the Iotic attitude when we consciously act in accordance with the Iotic principle. Acting in ignorance of Iota and its implications we might call *diotic*. Deliberately harming or planning to harm any part of Nature we might call *idiotic*. When I forget that to hurt others is to hurt myself, I am held captive by the diotic attitude, my peace of mind is diminished and conflict of some sort, whether internal or external, mental or physical, results. When I remember that I am in Iota and Iota is in me, I am set free: I am at peace with myself and the universe. Maintaining the Iotic attitude is a skill that can be learnt. But becoming entirely one with Iota is only fully achieved on death, when my temporary self is taken back into Iota, the infinite and eternal I.

*The most important implication of Iota.* Because we are all one, there are no individual selves, only the single infinite Self. This concept is all we need as a basis for how we should live. It reduces religious disagreements to absurdity, cuts down the impenetrable hedges of the moral maze and provides the means to solve all questions of ethics and morality. All we have to bear in mind is that when we do damage to others, we do damage to the Self of which we are finite and temporary modes. When we make war on others we make war on ourselves. When we torture others we torture ourselves. When we deceive others, we deceive ourselves. When we condemn others we condemn ourselves. When we act unjustly in any way we do injustice to ourselves.

*Belief in Iota.* There is no need to believe in Iota, any more than there is a need to believe in gravity or fresh air. But when we ignore or deny the Iotic principle then, just as when we ignore gravity or fresh air, we do so at our peril.

*Embracing Iota.* Acceptance that we are all one in Iota requires no baptism, no circumcision, no bar mitzvah, no church attendance or obedience to any form of religious doctrine whatsoever. It uses no fear of punishment or reward in an after-life to cajole people to accept it or believe in it. Iota is the natural, instinctive humanist philosophy that unifies rather than divides, banishes anxiety and allows people to develop their potential to the full.

Absolutist religion divides, discourages and imprisons; Iota unites, encourages and sets free.

*The single, enduring principle.* All that is good about religion – or any organization or community – is in accordance with Iota, and all that is bad comes about as a result of diotic or idiotic behavior. Whenever the principal of the single, infinite self is ignored, ill-will results. This applies universally, whether in the Cabinet office, the golf club, the synagogue, the Oval office, the mosque, the village hall or the kitchen.

*Iota and pacifism.* The principle of Iota accords with the principles of humanism and pacifism. Just as no sane person would take up arms against members of their own family, so no one who has grasped the Iotic principle can be anything but humanist and pacifist.

*Iota and Brahman.* The Upanishads teach belief in a world soul and a universal spirit, Brahman. Brahman can be compared to Iota: it is the ultimate, infinite existence, the sum total of all that ever is, was, or shall be. Brahman is not God in the monotheistic sense as it has no limiting characteristics. This monist philosophy, which is named *advaita*, 'not two', coheres with the concept of Iota as the infinite One.

*Buddhism and Iota.* The precepts of Buddhism are very much in accordance with the Iotic attitude. They are not given as commands in the form 'thou shalt not', but are guidelines to help us live a life in which one is happy, peaceful and without mental conflict. They are:

1. To refrain from taking life.
2. To refrain from taking that which is not given.
3. To refrain from sexual misconduct.
4. To refrain from lying.
5. To refrain from using drugs or alcohol.

*Qi and Iota.* In Chinese culture Qi is the life force that permeates the universe and is part of every living thing. If we recognize that everything that is, is Qi, or energy flow, it is easy to see that the concepts of Qi and Iota are closely allied.

*The insidiously damaging doctrine of original sin.* One of the fundamental differences between oriental and absolutist religions is that the former proclaim that the newborn baby is in every way perfect and unblemished, while the latter bring up their children to believe that they are stained from birth by original sin. The negative psychological effect of this doctrine is immeasurable. It is destructive of an individual's self-confidence and self-worth; it engenders breast-beating self-deprecation and fawning humility, and, perhaps worst of all, it provides people with a life-long excuse for 'falling by the wayside'.

The irrational and pernicious doctrine of original sin is the bedrock foundation of the Christian religion. Without it, the Gospel message would be meaningless.

*Personification of good and evil.* The ancient Greeks did not believe in any god that personified good or evil. Their gods were not separate from Nature but were part of Nature. As such they were readily comprehensible to human beings, who could not only enjoy the stories Homer and Hesiod told about them, but could learn from those stories. The concept of absolute evil personified by Satan (or Lucifer), together with the concept of absolute perfection personified by Jesus Christ (or Mohammed) has served to divide rather than unite the human race.

*Love thy neighbor.* The commandment 'love thy neighbor as thyself' comes close to the Iotic attitude, which takes it for granted that I and my neighbor are modes, or ways of being, of Iota. On that basis, if I am not at peace with others (i.e. if I do not love others) I cannot be at peace with myself, which is to say I cannot be happy. This applies equally to the individual, the family, the tribe, the township and the nation.

*A recipe for survival.* The next evolutionary leap forward for the human species will be the recognition that our survival depends upon our collective ability to think and act rationally. In particular, there must come about a universal realization that war is futile and that the species must co-operate if it is to survive. Whether that leap forward will take place seems very doubtful.

*Incompatibility of war with a just society.* Any nation-state that invades, threatens or prepares to make war on another sovereign state cannot be at peace with itself, nor can its people.

*Iotic altruism.* Once we have grasped that we are inescapably parts and parcels of Iota, and that hurting others hurts ourselves, all the problems of moral philosophy – 'how we should act' – vanish. We no longer need to think in terms of earning rewards for ourselves in a supposed afterlife. We are set free from the thou-shalt-not's of religious ethics. Our eyes are opened to the fact that it is not only to our advantage to act honestly, lovingly and peacefully and to regard others as extensions of our self, but that it would be folly to act in any other way.

*Theft as the only wrong.* All wrongdoing can be reduced to one form or other of theft, whether it is theft of life, theft of health, theft of livelihood, theft of a person's good name, theft of peace of mind, theft of self-confidence, theft of self-respect, theft of human rights, or theft of possessions.

*The Socratic consolation.* In the long run, it is better to be wronged and have no redress than to do wrong and suppose that one gets away with it. While a victim of crime can have peace of mind, that is never possible for the criminal.

*Revenge.* We do not make a bad man better by doing something bad to him. In taking or trying to take revenge, we turn ourselves into wrongdoers, and motivate other wrongdoers to take revenge upon us.

*The tradition of monism.* The conviction that all is one stretches back into pre-history and has survived repeated attempts by the leaders of absolutist religions (particularly Judaism, Christianity and Islam) to stamp it out. In Western philosophy it is found in the writings of the pre-Socratic mystic Parmenides, in the Stoic writings of Chrysippus, in Spinoza's *Ethics*, in Oersted's physics, in Faraday's metaphysical speculations, in the writings of Göethe, in the evolutionary science of Charles Darwin and in the relativity of Einstein. Quantum mechanics can only be approached by the intellect through a prior rejection of the supposition that the past, present and future are separate, or that there can be absolute points in space, absolute moments in time or absolute simultaneity of events.

*The impossibility of a mind-independent universe.* Descartes claimed that the universe could, through mathematics and geometry, ultimately be described to its last detail. His claim lives on in the 21st century in the belief that a Theory of Everything can be constructed. But it is a false claim, because it rides on the assumption that the human mind can 'step outside' the universe and describe it objectively: it presupposes the possibility of a mind that is independent of reality, and that there can be what has been called a 'view from nowhere'. But there is no 'nowhere' or view from it, nor can reality be mind-independent, for the simple reason that mind is part of reality. Nothing can have reality if it is outside reality. Things are either real or not real. If they stand outside reality, they are unreal. They are not.

*Parmenides and nothingness.* If individual things were to exist entirely separate from one another they would have to be separated by 'that which is not' or 'nothingness'. But nothingness is the negation of existence. It does not and cannot exist. So if we assert that individual things are separated by nothing, we say, in effect, that they are not separated at all.

In Parmenides' mystical poem, the goddess Justice instructs him in a way that 'lies apart from the path trodden by man' and forbids him to speak of 'that which is not', warning him that to do so will inevitably lead to illusion and falsehood:

> All that remains to be declared is the path It Is. On this path, there are many signposts: that What Is was never created and will never pass away, that it is single, whole, unmoved, eternal. It never 'was', it never 'will be' but Is Now, integral, one, continuous. What origin could you hope to find for it? What could it have evolved from? I forbid you to say or think that it comes from nothingness, which can be neither spoken of nor thought about: for it is not.

This passage has important implications. The first is that we should never attempt to make out that things are other than what they are. This is not merely a directive not to tell lies. It forbids us to disguise or dress up the truth in any way. It is a directive that prohibits all arguments that are presented in such a way as to convince people of something that is not altogether and wholly true, or that try to make something appear to be other than it is. The second implication is that all is one. It is a monumentally significant claim to make, because if all is one, then there can be no separate minds, only Mind. All science, all philosophy, and all knowledge must be one, as must the past, the present, and the future; and if time is one, events must also be all one so that causes cannot be separated from effects, and the assumption that we have free will and can influence events in the 'future' must be unfounded. The last implication is the most important. If all is one, then what we call 'God' must be one with all that is, and we have to admit that God and the universe, or Nature, are also one.

*Sartre and nothingness.* The problem with dualism is that it always forces us to presuppose some sort of gap of 'nothingness' between individual entities or substances. Such a gap then becomes a third sort of being in its own right: some even suggest that God *is* that gap. In *Being and Nothingness* Sartre makes a fatal mistake in supposing that being is grounded in nothingness. He is then faced with the problem of discussing the origin of nothingness. The result is nonsensical: 'The Being by which Nothingness arrives in the world,' he tells us, 'is a being such that in its Being, the Nothingness of its Being is in question.'

*The fruits of dualism.* Thinking dualistically always results in contradiction, and contradiction always results in conflict of some sort, whether logical, philosophical, political, religious or psychological. Descartes has much to answer for in this respect. He argues that the relationship between mind and matter must be a closer one than that between a sailor and his boat. But he insists not only that mind and matter are separate substances, but that a third substance, the infinite substance, or God, also exists. In doing so, he disobeys the goddess Justice in that he supposes a gap of nothingness between mind and matter. According to Descartes, mind *is not* matter, and God *is not* mind or matter but stands apart from both, in the same way that an artificer stands apart from his artefact.

*The search for origins.* The project of developing a single unifying theory that answers the ultimate question about how the natural universe 'began' is doomed to failure, for the simple reason that any such theory would have to include a definition of its own axioms, the possibility of which Kurt Gödel has shown to be impossible. Apart from that, the universe did not begin. The physical universe is not a finite thing but an attribute of what is infinite – Iota. As such it can only be comprehended through itself. Being infinite, Iota has no beginning and no end. The search for the beginning of the universe is a search for something that does not exist.

*Impossibility of absolute objectivity.* However hard we try, we can never be absolutely objective. For that to be possible our thought processes would have to be independent of and absolutely separated from Iota. Because Iota is one and infinitely inclusive, any statement we make about the world is stained by our own existence within the world, with the consequence that we can never guarantee a scientific theory absolutely, in rather the same way that we can never guarantee that the presence of the observer and the apparatus used to observe quanta does not influence their behavior.

*Descriptive inadequacy of mathematics.* Objectivity can be approached exponentially through mathematics, but it can never be achieved absolutely. Consider, for example, differential calculus, which is used to calculate the rate of growth of one variable with respect to another. To take a very simple example, the differential $dy/dx$ of the linear equation $y = 4x$, is 4, which means that at any point on the graph $y = 4x$, for any unit increase in y, x is increasing by 4 units, in the same way that, when we climb a one-in-four hill we climb one foot vertically for every four feet horizontally. In this case, the constant 4 represents the slope or gradient of the line. The differential (dy/dx) of $y = x^3$ is $3x^2$, which means that at any point on the graph, y is increasing at a rate three times the square of x.

Now consider Einstein's equation $E = c^2m$ where E represents energy, $c^2$ is the constant (the speed of light squared) and m is the variable, mass. Taking the speed of light to be 300,000,000 meters per second, we can now say that $E = 300,000,000^2 \times m$. Differentiating E with respect to m (dE/dm) we find that for an increase of one metric unit of mass, the energy of that mass increases by a factor of $300,000,000^2$, or ninety thousand trillion (90,000,000,000,000,000). This 'exchange rate' is so huge (or infinitesimal, depending on whether you are exchanging mass for energy or vice versa) that conventional mathematics is defeated by it, and for calculations not involving such high velocities treats the speed of light as infinite.

*Incompleteness of arithmetic.* Kurt Gödel's first theorem states that for any consistent formal, computably enumerable theory 'G' that proves basic arithmetical truths, an arithmetical statement that is true but not provable in the theory can be constructed – which is to say that any effectively generated theory capable of expressing elementary arithmetic cannot be both consistent and complete.

What Gödel showed is that you can never create a complete and consistent finite list of mathematical axioms. Each time you add a statement as an axiom, there will always be other true statements that still cannot be proved as true, even with the new axiom. Furthermore if the system can prove that it is consistent, then it is inconsistent.

Gödel's incompleteness theorems kill off the possibility of mathematical absolutism, and with it the possibility of constructing in mathematical terms a Theory of Everything. We are driven to conclude that human knowledge is asymptotic, and that however many billions of dollars are spent on particle accelerators in attempts to recreate the conditions of the so-called big bang, no 'ultimate answer' will ever be found.

*Incompleteness of human reason.* In his *Treatise of Human Nature*, Hume argues that whenever we make a judgment with regard to knowledge or probability we must always assess, from past experience, the probable reliability of that judgment. For example, if we wish to make a judgment about the reliability of an intelligence report, we should first assess the reliability of intelligence reports in general as well as the reliability of the intelligence source. But that is not all. We must also apply the same rule to ourselves and assess our own ability to make assessments as to the reliability of intelligence reports and intelligence sources. But there then emerge further questions concerning our ability to assess our own ability to assess prior probabilities and so on *ad infinitum* so that 'all the rules of logic require a continual diminution and, at last, a total extinction of belief and evidence.' Hume suggests there must be some natural mechanism defending the mind from such deep scepticism. Our very inability to pursue such reflections protects us from it. But as in the case of his solution to the problem of inductive knowledge, this is a psychological hypothesis rather than a philosophical explanation.

*From plus infinity to minus infinity.* If mathematics were adequate to the task of describing the universe, we would expect that any function of x could in every case be represented graphically as one curve. But this is not so. Plotting the equation $y = 1/x$ graphically results in not one but two curves that appear to be totally separate. As the value of plus or minus x increases towards plus or minus infinity, the value of y decreases towards zero; and as the value of x approaches zero, y increases towards infinity:

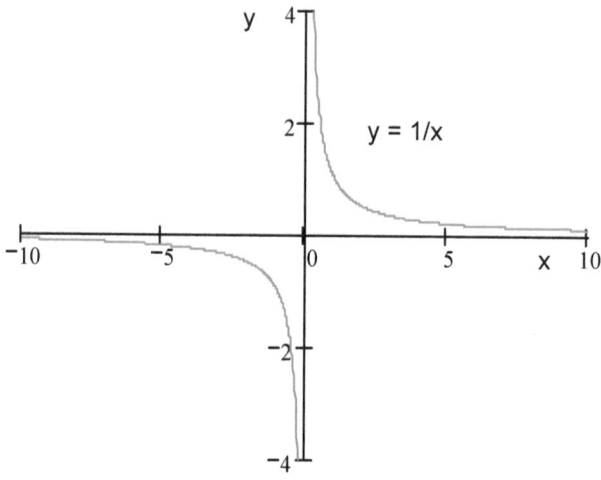

The result is two apparently separated curves, one in the first quadrant where all values of x and y are positive, and one in the third quadrant where all values of x and y are negative. The four 'ends' of these two curves zip away towards plus or minus infinity on one axis, and towards zero on the other.

If we could produce the axes to infinity, plus & minus x would be seen to be united on the x axis where x = plus & minus infinity, and plus & minus y would join on the y axis where y = plus & minus infinity. We should be left with a single, joined up figure, unified by infinity and separated by nothing, or zero.

Although it appears to us that there are two curves, in reality there is only one. The two apparent curves join at infinity and are separated on the graph by zero. Looking beyond mathematics, we might say that they are united by the infinite and separated by nothing. The two curves are one and infinite. In this way mathematics, through its own inadequacy, gives us a glimpse of Iota.

*The interaction between mind and body.* The mind-body problem is one of explaining how a non-physical thought can cause a part of the physical body to move, or how a physical event can cause a non-physical, mental event. What is going on when I raise my arm? Why am I excited by a thunderstorm? If mind and body are separate, there has to be a non-physical decision to raise my arm before the physical arm goes up: it doesn't just go up of its own accord; and the non-physical excitement that I experience during a thunderstorm has to be somehow linked to the physical discharge of electricity and the physical pressure waves caused by the clap of thunder.

If we claim that a non-physical thought causes the physical movement of the arm, and that a physical discharge of electricity causes the non-physical experience of excitement, there seems to be a causal gap between what is physical and what is non-physical: they must be interacting if we believe that the mind and body are separate, but cannot be interacting if we apply Newton's law, 'to every action an equal and opposite reaction'.

The problem vanishes as soon as we accept that mind and body are one, and that just as matter and energy are two aspects of, or ways of looking at, the universe, so are thought activity and physical activity two aspects of living beings, in the same way that a quantum of energy can be viewed now as a wave, and now as a particle.

*Free will.* 'In the mind there is no absolute, or free, will, but the mind is determined to will this is or that by a cause which is also determined by another, and this again by another, and so to infinity.' (Spinoza, *Ethics*)

While belief that we can make a choice 'of our own free will' seems to be necessary for the normal functioning of human existence, if we enquire into *why* and *how* we take a decision or make a choice, we find that such a decision or choice comes about as a result of an infinite network of causes. Consider, for instance, a seminar in philosophy being conducted at a university. The professor is enlarging upon Wittgenstein's *Philosophical Investigations*. He pauses to ask a question. One of the students raises a hand to indicate that he can answer. Now: a believer in 'free will' would contend that the decision to raise the hand was taken at an absolute moment in time, and that it preceded the actual raising of the hand. One moment the motor neurons would be inactive; the next, after operation of the will, a message has been transmitted from the brain to the muscles to make them raise the hand. With regard to the physical process of raising the arm we might (just possibly) suggest that three brain states are supposed: (1) free will inactive, (2) free will acting to raise arm, (3) free will acting to keep arm raised. That decision, that exercise of free will, must, if the will is truly free, be self-causing: as soon as we attribute a cause of that decision, the decision is no longer free: it is determined by a prior event.

But that is not all. The decision to raise the hand is caused, for example, not simply because the student knows the answer and wants to give it, but because he is present in the seminar room and the seminar room is there for him to be present in it. If we trace the student's history back through time, we shall, perhaps, find a few of the multiple reasons why he went to university and why he chose to study Wittgenstein's philosophy.

To be consistent, a believer in free will would have to claim that each step in his life was the result of decisions that he made of his own free will – he could not admit to the existence of any events that forced him into action that he did not previously will.

If we trace our imaginary student's life history back to infancy, we discover a time when he was not making any choices at all: every decision affecting his life was taken by someone else, principally his mother. Over time, he has been conditioned by his experience of life to look after himself and behave in ways that help him to survive as a sociable, civilized human being. Part of this conditioning includes the experience of pleasant and unpleasant consequences of actions, through which he learns to be a sociable creature. This particular student has, perhaps, been born of parents who have encouraged him to work hard at school, join in and better himself.

When we now return to the moment when the philosophy student 'decides' to raise his hand and answer the professor's question, we can see that far from doing so of his own free will, the raising of the hand and the answering of the question are infinitesimal events in the infinite and eternal network of events through which he is realized as a finite mode of Iota. The raising of the hand and the answering of the question are not isolated events but are themselves effects and causes of actions and thoughts of every member of the seminar as well as the professor conducting it. Nor is the raising of his hand causative of human actions only: perhaps it causes a fly to take off and buzz around the seminar room, breaking the professor's line of thought and prompting him to make an oblique reference to Wittgenstein's comparison of philosophers to a fly in a bottle, trying to get out. His remark causes some students to smile, and as a result he forms new judgments about them and they form new judgments about him, and some of those judgments will inevitably be partial causes of the future actions and behavior of everyone in the room.

When we are asleep or unconscious we have no free will at all. So the question must be asked, how does it become operative? How is it switched on? We do not wake up in the morning and make a decision 'of our own free will' to switch our free will on, nor do we decide 'of our own free will' to switch it off before falling asleep at night. As any insomniac knows, one can be kept awake for hours by thoughts that seem to bombard the mind.

Only Iota is free. As finite modes of Iota, we have a share in that freedom. The more completely we accept this, the more freedom we have, while the more we try to impose our will upon the world, the more frustrated we become. Free will is not freedom of the *individual* will, it is the freedom of Iota. Our free will is nothing more than a mode of Iota's free will.

*Free will and religious conditioning.* Belief in God comes about solely as a result of some sort of conditioning, the commonest form being superstitious or religious conditioning from infancy brought about as a result of arguments of persuasion and emotion rather than reason. As St. Ignatius of Loyola, the founder of the Society of Jesus put it: 'Give me the child for seven years, and I will give you the man.' We do not become Christian, Jewish or Muslim of our own free will: we are either born and brought up in those faiths or converted to them. Whichever is the case, a suspension of the rational faculty is involved.

*The unforeseeable future.* Even if we did have free will, it would only be useful to us if we could see into the future. But we cannot see into the future: we stumble backwards through time, aware only of events we have experienced in the past. We form judgments about the world, our place in it and how to act solely on the basis of *past* events and *past* experience. Such judgments are possible only because we have confidence that causes we have experienced in the past will have the same sort of effects in the future as we have experienced them as having in the past, and that when we make judgments based on conditional inferences, they are reliable.

*Sound judgment.* Arrogance is the enemy of sound judgment. The more firmly we believe in our own ability to control future events, the more likely we are to find that events control us, and that our aims and projects are frustrated. The only control we have is over ourselves, and that control comes about as a result of exercising our faculty of reason. Conflict and unhappiness are the inevitable consequences of failure (or refusal) to engage with reason.

*Conflict between utilitarianism and existentialism.* The utilitarian has to believe in free will and the ability of one human being to bring about happiness-or-pleasure for others. By contrast the existentialist regards human existence as a process of becoming what one is through what one does. Politicians write manifestos and create policies on the utilitarian principle of creating the greatest happiness for the greatest number; but they are judged existentially by the electorate on the consequences of their actions.

*Law of unforeseen consequences.* Dramatic irony is one of the most difficult effects to achieve in literature, and at the same time the most aesthetically satisfying when it is fully achieved. Its commonest form, perhaps, is the story of someone who sets out to bring about the downfall of a rival and in doing so unwittingly brings about his own downfall. This sort of drama is satisfying because it gives us a glimpse of Iota: the relentless, unceasing progression of necessary cause to necessary effect. It is both cathartic and educative. We recognize in ourselves the same character qualities or flaws as those of a hero or anti-hero; we are shown how a chain of ill-judged decisions made with one end in mind can result in the very opposite of the desired consequence. But in the most fully developed dramas it goes deeper than that. The human condition is revealed to us. We come away with the feeling that we have been given a glimpse not only of ourselves but of the infinite of which we are a part. In other words, we have been given a glimpse of Iota.

*Ask not for whom the bell tolls.* Ernest Hemingway's novel, *A Farewell to Arms* is a fine example of how literature can give us a glimpse of Iota. This is the story of a medic serving in Italy during World War I who, after being injured and hospitalised, falls in love with a nurse and makes her pregnant. They escape from the war by rowing across Lake Garda and, after passing an idyllic winter together, the nurse dies in childbirth. The poignancy of the last scene is almost unbearable, but at the same time uplifting. Through it, we are brought face to face with the triumph and tragedy of the human condition.

Hemingway's other war novel, *For Whom the Bell Tolls*, has a similar theme of love and sacrifice in war. It takes its title from a line in John Donne's *Meditation 17*, one of the most beautiful passages in the English language, which reflects the Iotic principle:

> All mankind is of one author and is one volume; when one man dies, one chapter is

not torn out of the book, but translated into a better language; and every chapter must be so translated. God employs several translators; some pieces are translated by age, some by sickness, some by war, some by justice; but God's hand is in every translation, and his hand shall bind up all our scattered leaves again for that library where every book shall lie open to one another. As therefore the bell that rings a sermon calls not upon the preacher only, but upon the congregation to come, so this bell calls us all; but how much more me, who am brought so near the door by this sickness. [...] The bell doth toll for him that thinks it doth; and though it intermit again, yet from that minute that that occasion wrought upon him, he is united to God. Who casts not up his eye to the sun when it rises? But who takes off his eye from a comet when that breaks out? Who bends not his ear to any bell which upon any occasion rings? But who can remove it from that bell which is passing a piece of himself out of this world? No man is an island, entire of itself; every man is a piece of the continent, a part of the main. If a clod be washed away by the sea, Europe is the less, as well as if a promontory were, as well as if a manor of thy friend's or of thine own were. Any man's death diminishes me, because I am involved in mankind; and therefore never send to know for whom the bell tolls; it tolls for thee.

*Karma and Iota.* In the Hindu, Jain, Sikh and Buddhist philosophies, karma is seen as the cause of the infinite cycle of cause and effect. The general concept of karma is closely aligned to the Iotic principle. It is that, because we are all one with each other, the effects of all deeds create past, present, and future experiences, thus making one responsible for all the pain or joy one's deeds bring to one's self and to others. In bringing about bad karma for others, we bring about bad karma for ourselves.

When things go wrong or we have bad luck or the law of unforeseen consequences seems to be operating, people sometimes say, 'Karma.' In the same way, when the reverse of what was intended comes about as a result of diotic reasoning or behavior, we might say, 'Iota.'

*God's will.* The belief that the universe was created by God presupposes that God existed before time began, and was cause of his own existence. On that supposition, creation of the universe was an act of will on God's part. Such an act could not have been determined in any way: it must have been an act of *free* will. Such a belief would be tenable if it could be left at that. But it is not left at that: theists invite us to believe not only that human beings have free will, but that their actions can be contrary to God's will – that on some occasions God's will is done and on others it is not done. This objection is supported by the thought that if God's will were *always* done, there would be no point in praying to him, and Jesus would not have taught his followers to pray, 'Thy will be done.'

*How God abdicated his own free will.* Some sort of creation story has to be believed in order to believe in a theistic God. Even if we dismiss as a myth the creation story in the book of Genesis, we still have to believe that God existed prior to the creative event. But this throws up a contradiction about the supposed nature of God which is seldom addressed. Belief in theism necessitates belief that before time began, God's will was absolute and could not be contravened, but that since the creation of the human species, God's will can be contravened. What has happened here? A description of the nature of God before the beginning of time would have to attribute to him a will that could not be contravened; but after creation, a description of the nature of God would have to attribute the ability of the human race to contravene God's will. So it seems that we are being invited to believe in a God who has brought about in himself a fundamental and catastrophic change. Once upon a time his will was absolute and could not be contravened; but once upon a later time his will can be contravened. In creating the human species, he seems to have re-created himself as a lesser god, whose will is no longer absolute, but can be contravened by the beings he created 'of his own free will'.

*Conflict between the human will and the will of God.* Belief in free will is fundamental to the Christian belief that human beings are essentially different from all other members of the animal kingdom. Without the belief that God gave human beings free will, together with the ability to differentiate between good and evil, the Gospel story loses all coherence and foundation; but that same belief is logically incompatible with belief in an omnipotent God, as the will of such a God could not possibly be transgressed by one of his creatures. We are, effectively, being invited to believe that a once omnipotent God with absolute free will has re-created himself in such a way as to be *not* omnipotent, having a will that is *not* free in that it can be wilfully obstructed by the free will of human beings.

*Let this cup pass from me.* The supposed conflict between the will of God and human will is vividly exemplified by the account of Jesus in the garden of Gethsemane:

> And he went a little further, and fell on his face, and prayed, saying, O my Father, if it be possible, let this cup pass from me: nevertheless not as I will, but as thou wilt.
>
> (Matt. 26: 39)

This short passage throws up a number of questions with regard to the will and omnipotence of God and the divinity of Jesus Christ. If Jesus' claim 'I and the father are one' (John 10: 30) is to be believed, how can a single divinity (God the Father and God the Son) have two conflicting wills? Wasn't Jesus aware that 'with God all things are possible' (Matt. 19: 26)? And how do we know that Jesus prayed in this way? Did he come back and tell the disciples what he had just prayed? Or did he pray out loud so that they could hear what he was saying? In which case, was someone taking notes? Or is this a case of the author of the Gospel making up the story decades later, not realizing that he was building into it a fatal contradiction?

*Wisdom and folly; good and evil.* Right and wrong can be differentiated in the same way as wisdom and folly. Right is to wrong as wisdom is to folly, and as knowledge is to ignorance. The Iotic principle serves as an infallible guide to discerning what is wise from what is folly, and consequently good from evil. However, observance of the Iotic principle necessitates the operation of reason and the rejection of arguments of persuasion.

*Divine commands.* The Ten Commandments of the Mosaic Law are the products of human wisdom. They were designed for the purpose of maintaining law and order and social cohesion among the children of Israel. Moses and Aaron needed to instil belief in a single, absolute and almighty God with whom they were in direct touch in order to establish their authority as leaders having the ability to interpret and pass on divine commands. Kings, emperors, dictators, politicians, popes, ayatollahs and political and religious leaders have used the same trick down the centuries, and continue to do so today.

Because no divinity exists, there can be no divine commands, only the commands of those in authority who claim to be in contact with an imaginary divinity.

*Evolution of religious belief.* Belief in spirits, whether evil or good, predates polytheistic belief by many thousands of years. Such spirits were regarded as part of nature, and in some primitive societies continue to be so regarded. Long before the Greeks gave their gods names and attributed separate responsibilities for parts of creation to them, nameless spirits were believed to inhabit plant and animal life forms and to be involved in every event that affected human life. Because mankind depended so heavily on nature for survival, it seemed prudent to regard nature and the spirits believed to inhabit it with respect. Even today it is common practice in certain parts of the world for hunters to pay homage to the spirit of the animal they have killed for food.

Floods, earthquakes, famines and other disasters came about, it was believed, as a result of the actions of spirits. Inevitably, individual spirits were given names and were associated with different parts of nature. But the Greeks did not regard the gods as creators who stood in an absolute relation to the universe, as do Christians, Muslims and Jews. The Greek gods were a part of nature and interacted within it. Homer and Hesiod established the gods as having individual characters, with flaws and qualities with which human beings readily identified.

In Rome at the time of Christ there were two principal religious disagreements. One was between those who believed there were many gods and those who believed there was only one god; the other was between those (principally the Stoics) who identified Zeus (or God) with Nature, and those (principally the Jews) who believed that Jehovah (or God) stood apart from, and in an absolute relationship to, Nature.

The advent of Christianity effectively killed off Stoic religion and with it the belief that God and Nature could be one and the same thing. One thousand eight hundred years later, when, thanks chiefly to Charles Darwin, the evidence for an evolved world became overwhelming, the return to the idea that the natural world is all there is enabled scientists to make giant leaps forward in biology and physics.

*Intelligent design.* The last refuge of theologians is to claim that Nature is the product of 'intelligent design', a concept that slips easily through the fingers when we try to catch it by the tail. It is one of theology's silly ideas, a metaphysical speculation that when examined at the most superficial level is revealed as nonsense.

For there to be a design, there has to be a designer, and a design on its own, without an artisan or manufacturer, produces nothing. The claim that Nature is the product of intelligent design prompts two unanswerable questions: first, 'Of what was intelligent design the product?' And second, 'By what agent was the universe manufactured in accordance with intelligent design?' To give an answer to the first question we should have to suppose a creator of the design; to answer the second, we should have to suppose a manufacturer who used the design to put the universe together. We therefore end up with three mystical persons or agencies: the creator of intelligent design, the intelligent design itself, and the supernatural artisan who refers to the design to put the universe together and oversee its evolutionary development.

*The Euthyphro conundrum.* Plato's project in the *Euthyphro* is to draw attention to the inconsistencies involved in believing the Homeric stories about the gods, who are depicted as displaying human emotions and behaving in ways that the state of Athens held to be impious. In the fifth century BCE, obedience to the laws of Athens was deemed to be part of a pious, religious life. A citizen was law-abiding if and only if he was pious. If murder was committed, the murderer was said to be polluted and offensive to the gods. The punishment for such an offence meted out by the state was believed to have a purifying as well as deterrent effect. Lawful acts were those that were pleasing to the gods, and piety consisted in obeying the law. But what, Socrates asks in Plato's dialogue *Euthyphro,* is piety *in itself?*

Plato makes comparisons between three different levels of relationship: child to parent, citizen to state, and mortals to the gods. The dialogue is set in Athens just before Socrates is due to stand trial on a charge of impiety. Outside the court, Socrates bumps into Euthyphro, who claims to be an expert on matters of piety and the law. Socrates is shocked to hear that Euthyphro intends to prosecute his own father on a charge of murder, the victim of which was also a murderer. Euthyphro justifies his decision by pointing out that Zeus, the best and most righteous of all the gods, punished his own father by putting him in chains. Such an act seems contradictory in that it runs counter to the human instinct of love and respect for one's father yet is performed by the god regarded – and referred to – as the 'Heavenly Father'. Socrates is pointing out that Zeus is acting like a tyrant, saying in effect, 'Don't do as I do, do as I tell you.'

Socrates asks Euthyphro to explain to him not only why it is pious, (or obedient to the state and the gods) to prosecute one's own father in such circumstances but what piety really *is*. Euthyphro suggests that piety consists of doing what the gods want. Prompted by Socrates, he agrees that piety is 'what *all* the gods love' and impiety is 'what *all* the gods hate'. The emphasis on *all* is deliberate. Plato is taking for granted that his listeners know very well that, if Homer's and Hesiod's stories about them are to be believed, the gods are seldom in unanimous agreement and have a disreputable history of misbehavior, promiscuity, conflict and violence. But that is not the only objection to Euthyphro's definition of piety because Socrates wants Euthyphro, the self-styled expert, to give him a model or universal form for piety so that he will always be able to know what is pious and what is not pious. Having posed the question and suggested an answer, Socrates then proceeds to tie Euthyphro in dialectical knots:

'So we don't see a thing because it is a seen thing, but on the contrary it is a seen thing because we see it; and we don't lead a thing because it is a led thing, but it is a led thing because we lead it; and we don't carry a thing because it is a carried thing, but it is a carried thing because we carry it.'

When Euthyphro agrees with this, Socrates leads him into a trap: 'Then what do we say about piety?

Isn't it loved by all the gods, according to your definition?'

'Yes.'

'Just because it is pious, not pious because it is loved?'

'It seems so.'

'But it is because a thing is loved by the gods that it is an object of love, or god-beloved.'

'Of course.'

'Then what is god-beloved is not the same as what is pious, Euthyphro, nor is what is pious the same as what is god-beloved, as you assert; they are two different things.'

'Then is everything that is morally right pious?' Socrates asks Euthyphro, 'Isn't the truth that, although what is pious is morally right, what is morally right is not all pious, but some of it is pious and some is something else?'

Socrates suggests that piety is a sort of trade between gods and mortals in which mortals pander to the wishes of the gods and, in return, the gods pander to the wishes of mortals. But this explanation seems to be making fun of a serious subject, and Euthyphro uses the time-honored trick of politicians who don't want to answer awkward questions by telling Socrates that he doesn't have time to go on talking, and walks out of the interview.

*The dangerous question.* Do we worship God because we believe in him, or do we believe in him because we worship him? This question forces the believer to the edge of an abyss, because whether we answer that we worship because we believe or that we believe because we worship, we are then faced with questions concerning the reason *why* we believe or worship, the only truthful answer to which is that we do so not as a result of rational choice but because we have been brought up or persuaded to do so.

*The false foundations of theology.* An *a priori* idea is one that is said to exist in the mind before experience. All theology is founded on the *a priori* idea that a supernatural God exists. However, to believe in any *a priori* idea it is first necessary to believe another *a priori* idea, namely that such ideas are possible. But it is impossible to prove that they exist, so belief in a supernatural divinity is based on belief in the presence of ideas said to be implanted in us supernaturally but whose existence it is impossible to prove from experience.

From this we can conclude that all theology is based on belief in an infinity of unfounded beliefs – or, to put it more bluntly, falsehoods.

*Vain repetition.* As every religious leader – or leader who is religious – knows, the more often you can get people to repeat prayers, chant responses, sing hymns and read out texts from scriptures that have been declared holy, the stronger becomes their belief, and the more slavishly automatic their obedience to the discipline of their teachers. From the earliest times to the present day, kings, tyrants, popes, ayatollahs, rabbis, pastors, politicians and witch doctors have used mankind's liking for ceremony and legends about paradise for 'us' and hell for 'them' to bring the common people into obedient subjection.

*Crime, sin and punishment.* A crime is an act that contravenes the laws of the state. A sin is an act that contravenes the laws of religion. The former is punishable by the state. The latter is supposedly punishable by God. Punishment by the state, however severe, is more just than supposed punishment by God, as the former comes to an end but the latter is eternal.

*Morals and ethics.* Strictly speaking, ethics are norms of behavior legislated by a state, while morals are universal, unwritten standards of humane behavior conventionally agreed. On those definitions, it is possible to behave ethically but not morally, and to behave morally but not ethically. For instance, female circumcision is deemed ethical in certain cultures and religions, including at least one sect of Islam, but causes moral revulsion in the mind of any human being who is not under the sway of authoritarian culture or religion.

*Sin and divine punishment.* If we believe that God is omnipresent, punishment for the 'sin' of any individual will necessarily imply punishment of a creature in which God resides – in other words punishment of God by God. To believe in eternal punishment is to believe that God punishes himself eternally. The idea put forward by some preachers that hell is 'separation from God' contradicts the fundamental beliefs of those same preachers in that it presupposes the possibility of absolute separation from an omnipresent being.

*Original sin.* Original sin is said to have resulted in the Fall of Man, when Adam and Eve ate the forbidden fruit of a particular tree in the Garden of Eden. This first sin is traditionally understood – by Jews, Christians and Muslims – to be the cause of the 'fallen' state of humanity. In addition to Adam and Eve's disobedience, their action was preceded by a decision not to believe what God had told them, namely that they would die if they ate of the fruit of this particular tree. Satan, in the form of a snake, told them that what God had said was not true. Adam and Eve chose to believe Satan's version of the facts rather than believing in what God had said.

*Inconsistency of the creation myth.* No myth, legend or allegory can serve a useful moral purpose if it is not consistent; and the story of the Garden of Eden is not consistent, as it invites us to believe that an all-knowing, all-powerful and all-present God created human beings in the full knowledge that they would disobey him, and that he would punish them for behaving in the way he created them to behave. To believe in original sin one has to ignore the fact that, being omniscient and omnipotent, God must have known from all eternity that things would go horribly wrong.

*God in the dock.* If the actions and decisions of the god of the creation story in the book of Genesis were to be subject to a civil court of enquiry, there would be good grounds for indictment: first, that God abused his omnipotence and omniscience in knowingly and deliberately creating beings in his own likeness with the fundamental flaw of original sin; second, that he allowed this flawed being to continue in existence when he could have made it extinct and started anew, and third, that he compounded the misery of humans by creating in them the fear of eternal punishment. These are the actions of a wicked and cruel tyrant, not of a loving and merciful God. Within the context of the creation story, if there was any original sin, it was neither Man's, nor Satan's – it was God's.

*The trick Prometheus played on Zeus.* There are obvious parallels between the mythical conflict between Jehovah and Satan in the book of Genesis, and the

Greek legend of the conflict between Zeus and Prometheus, which predates the Mosaic account by hundreds of years.

Zeus was known for erotic escapades which resulted in many divine offspring, including Athena, Apollo, Artemis, Hermes, Persephone, Aphrodite, Dionysus, Perseus, Heracles, Helen, Minos, Ares, Hebe and Hephaestus. In the *Theogony*, Hesiod introduces Prometheus as a challenger to the omniscience and omnipotence of Zeus.

The trouble started when Prometheus played 'trick or treat' with Zeus. He placed two sacrificial offerings before him: a selection of ox meat hidden inside an ox's stomach: 'nourishment hidden inside a displeasing exterior' and ox bones wrapped in glistening fat: 'something inedible hidden inside a pleasing exterior'. Zeus was tricked into choosing the latter, and in doing so a precedent was set. In future humans would continue the tradition by keeping the meat for themselves, while the bones wrapped in fat were to be a sacrificial offering to the gods. And so the barbecue tradition originated. Zeus was so angry with Prometheus for playing a trick on him that he hid fire from humans in retribution, whereupon Prometheus stole fire from Zeus and gave it back to humans. That further enraged Zeus, who sent the first woman, Pandora, into the world. 'From her is the race of women and female kind: of her is the deadly race and tribe of women who live amongst mortal men to their great trouble, no helpmeets in hateful poverty.' In addition to giving humankind fire, Prometheus is said to have taught the arts of civilization – writing, mathematics, medicine, agriculture and science, in the same way that Satan is said to have persuaded Adam and Eve to eat the fruit of the tree of knowledge. In *Prometheus Bound*, the Greek tragedy attributed to Aeschylus, he is characterised as the son of God who is the benefactor and savior of humanity. His punishment of being nailed to a rock bears a striking resemblance to the crucifixion.

*The justice of Zeus and the justice of God.* It could be argued that, having been tricked by Prometheus, Zeus acted justly in punishing Prometheus; but when it is remembered that within the context of the Genesis story Adam and Eve were God's creatures whose frailties and infirmities must have been known by God from all eternity, God's treatment of them appears as cruelly unjust. From the outset, the God of Abraham, Isaac and Ishmael reveals himself as an anti-woman shape-shifter, who offloads responsibility for the catastrophic consequences of his creative actions onto the shoulders of humankind.

*Where Jesus got his ideas.* In deliberately behaving in a way that he knew must inevitably lead to crucifixion, was Jesus deliberately acting out ideas gleaned from Greek mythology and the life of Socrates? Did he see that the influence of Socrates lay in the fact that he was executed for his beliefs, and by going willingly and cheerfully to his death on the grounds that his soul was immortal he took the sting out of death and scored a victory over the grave? Did he see that if he offered himself as a sacrifice on the cross people would immortalise him just as Prometheus, who was nailed to a rock, had been immortalised? Was the whole project of claiming to be the son of God and offering himself as a sacrifice for the redemption of man's original sin inspired by a popular myth that had been around for a thousand years?

*Orphism.* The myth of Orpheus bears a striking resemblance to the Christian gospel story. Both are characterized by a woman's involvement with a snake, her disobedience to the authority of a male divinity, a place of eternal punishment and the coming of a beautiful, talented young man who suffers on behalf of others, descends into hell, rises again, ascends into heaven and is worshipped as a god.

The famous story in which Orpheus figures is that of his wife Eurydice, who, while fleeing from Aristaeus, the son of Apollo, ran into a nest of snakes which bit her legs and killed her. (Cf. Genesis 3: 14-15: 'And the Lord God said unto the serpent, Because thou hast done this, thou art cursed above all cattle, and above every beast of the field; upon thy belly shalt thou go, and dust shalt thou eat all the days of thy life: And I will put enmity between thee and the woman, and between thy seed and her seed; it shall bruise thy head, and thou shalt bruise his heel.') Distraught, Orpheus played such sad songs on his lyre that the gods wept. On their advice, Orpheus traveled to the underworld and by his music softened the hearts of Hades. Eurydice was allowed to return to Earth with Orpheus on the condition that he must walk in front of her and not look back until they both reached the upper world. In his anxiety for her safety, he forgot Persephone's condition and turned back to look at her, whereupon she vanished.

The descent to the Underworld of Orpheus is paralleled in other versions of a worldwide theme: the Japanese myth of Izanagi and Izanami, the Sumerian myth of Inanna's descent to the underworld, the Mayan myth of Ix Chel and Itzamna – and, most obviously, the myth of Jesus Christ descending into hell, rising again, and ascending to heaven.

The theme of not looking back is reflected in the story in the Old Testament of Lot's wife, who looked back when escaping from Sodom and was turned into a pillar of salt. When it is remembered that Pandora is blamed in Greek mythology for opening her box and releasing diseases into the world, that Eve is blamed for tempting Adam, that the apostle Paul directed that women should keep silent in the church, and that right across the Islamic world women are oppressed and disempowered – and in some cases cruelly circumcised in childhood – it seems that throughout history religious leaders have demonstrated an obsessive need to bring down divine blame upon women for many of the ills that attend humanity.

*The death of Orpheus.* According to a summary of Aeschylus's lost play *Bassarids*, Orpheus adopted monotheism at the end of his life: he turned his back on all the gods save Apollo, who stands for sober authority, wisdom and science. One morning Orpheus went to the oracle of Dionysus – who stands for rebellious art, music and dance – to salute Appollo. Ovid recounts that the Thracian Maenads, Dionysus' followers, angry for having been spurned by Orpheus, tore him to pieces during the frenzy of a Bacchic orgy. His head and lyre, still singing mournful songs, floated down the Hebrus to the Mediterranean, where the winds carried them over to Lesbos. There, the inhabitants buried his head, and a shrine was built in his honor near Antissa. His lyre was carried to heaven by the Muses, and was placed among the stars.

Another account of his death is that he was struck by lightning by Zeus for having revealed the mysteries of the gods to men – rather in the same way that Zeus/God punished Prometheus/Lucifer/Satan for doing much the same thing. The conflict between Apollo and Dionysus, and the rejection by Plato and Socrates of the rebellious, free-thinking Dionysian attitude in favor of the self-effacing, conscience-stricken attitude of 'Socratism', is the theme of Nietzsche's *The Birth of Tragedy*.

*The influence of Orphism on the Roman Catholic Church.* It seems likely that the Roman Catholic Church took on and adapted some of the ceremonies and practices of Orphism. The Mysteries of the Holy Rosary may have been inspired by the Orphic Mysteries; the practice of confining virgins in convents may have found its origin in the vestal virgins of Orphism.

*The offer that can't be refused.* At birth we all share a common, unsullied humanity. It is only teaching and indoctrination that divides us from one another and sets us at enmity with those who do not believe what we have been brought up to believe, or do not observe the customs we are accustomed to observe. Until it is stamped out of us by politico-religious indoctrination, we share an innate sense of justice that applies across race and religion to all human beings. Absolutist religion, by its very nature, is in conflict with that sense, in that it teaches its adherents to believe that an infinitely powerful creator is so immoral and unjust as to punish some of his creatures and reward others. This inhuman threat – this Mafia-like offer that cannot be refused – is still used to frighten people into political or religious subjection and to motivate conflict.

*Triumph of humanity over religion.* In Percy Bysshe Shelley's *Prometheus Unbound*, Prometheus refuses to submit to Zeus, but supplants him instead in a triumph of the human heart and intellect over tyrannical religion. Byron's poem *Prometheus* also portrays Prometheus as unrepentant. For the Romanticists of the 19th century, Prometheus was the rebel who resisted all forms of institutional tyranny epitomized by church, monarch and patriarch.

*The Lucifer myth.* The name Lucifer means 'light-bearer'. The Hebrew equivalent, Helel ben Shahar, means 'dawn-bearer'. The Book of Isaiah (14: 12) refers to one of the titles of a Babylonian King: 'How art thou fallen from Heaven, O Lucifer, son of the morning! How art thou come down to the ground, which didst weaken the nations! For thou hast said in thine heart, I will ascend into heaven, I will exhort my throne above the stars of God: I will sit also upon the mount of the congregation, in the sides of the North: I will ascend above the heights of the clouds: I will be like the Most High.'

Later interpretations of the text, as well as the influence of Dante's *Inferno* and Milton's *Paradise Lost,* led to the interpretation that Lucifer was a poetic appellation of Satan. Christian thought derived from this interpretation the idea that Lucifer is a fallen angel, the embodiment of evil and the enemy of God, in much the same way that that Prometheus was seen as an enemy of Zeus. In Christian literature, Lucifer is considered to have been a prominent archangel in heaven, although the Book of Ezekiel (28: 14-18) says:

> You were the anointed cherub who covereth, and I have set thee so: thou wast upon the holy Mountain of God; thou hast walked up and down in the midst of the stones of fire. Thou wast perfect in thy ways from the day that thou wast created, till iniquity was found in thee. By the multitude of thy merchandise they have filled the midst of thee with violence, and thou hast

sinned: therefore, I will cast thee as profane out of the Mountain of God: and I will destroy thee, O covering cherub, from the midst of the stones of fire. Thine heart was lifted up because of thy beauty; thou hast corrupted thy wisdom by reason of thy brightness: I will cast thee to the ground, I will leave you before kings, that they may behold thee. Thou hast defiled thy sanctuaries by the multitude of thine iniquities, by the iniquity of thy traffic; therefore will I bring forth a fire from the midst of thee; it shall devour thee; and I will bring thee to ashes upon the earth, in the sight of all them that behold thee.

*The War of Heaven.* In the story of the War of Heaven, Lucifer is motivated by pride to lead a revolution against God. When the rebellion fails, Lucifer is cast out of heaven, along with a third of the heavenly host, and comes to reside on Earth. The event which drove Lucifer to make his unsuccessful coup was the creation of mankind, to whom God ordered all his angels to bow down. Lucifer considered this an insult and fomented discontent among other angels, who were God's first creation.

In the 13th Century the Bishop of Tusculum estimated that 133,306,666 angels took Lucifer's side leaving 266,613,336 who remained loyal to God. These figures were later confirmed by the 15th century scholar Alphonso de Spina.

*Canonization of the books of the Bible.* The canonization of the twenty-four books of the Tanakh or Hebrew Bible probably took place over several hundreds of years between 200 BCE and 200 CE. It was conducted principally by Pharisees, who decided which books to include and which to exclude. Its authority and composition are therefore dependent on decisions made by self-appointed human committees. Belief in the authority of the Bible rests on the belief in the authority of Pharisees to whom Jesus referred as a 'generation of vipers' – and in doing so cast doubt upon the authority of the old Testament.

The canonization of the New Testament was a similarly slow process that was finalised at the Council of Trent in the mid-16th century. Once again, in order to believe any part of it we must first put our faith in the authority of those human beings who decided which books to include and which to exclude, and who declared it to be the inspired word of God.

In the case of the Qu'ran and the Old and New Testaments of the Bible, we have to put our faith in the ability of translators, the competence of the scribes and the truthfulness of the authors and editors. Many works were excluded from the Bible because they were deemed theologically incorrect by pharisees or bishops, and the presence of many lacunae in early manuscripts rendered it almost impossible to reproduce the original meaning of the text with any degree of certainty. The earliest known manuscript of the Qu'ran is written in a kind of shorthand, in which important dots are omitted, with the result that the seventy-two houris promised to faithful Muslims in Paradise can be alternatively translated as a bunch of grapes.

*Essence of the Christian gospel.* The books of the New Testament as canonized by the Church of Rome contain all the information needed to embrace the Christian faith, which can be summarised as follows:

1. Man is naturally sinful – Romans 8: 1-7
2. and is spiritually dead – Ephesians 2: 1

3. Being convicted of sin – Luke 15: 18
4. he repents – Matthew 21: 28-29
5. and confesses his sin to Christ – John, 1: 9
6. He is then redeemed – 1 Peter 1: 18-19
7. by the propitiatory sacrifice of Jesus Christ – Galatians 3: 13
8. through faith – Ephesians 2: 8
9. in his blood – Romans 3: 23-25
10. and is forgiven – 1 John 1: 9
11. and justified – Romans 4, and 5: 1
12. He becomes regenerate – 2 Corinthians 5: 1
13. Having accepted eternal life by faith as a gift – Romans 6: 23
14. and is sanctified – 2 Corinthians 5: 20
15. by the Holy Spirit – 1 Corinthians 3: 16
16. who delivers from sin – Romans 6: 14
17. gives victory over temptation – 1 Corinthians 10: 13
18. helps to serve and glorify God – John 15: 8.
19. He watches for Christ's return – Mark 13: 34-37
21. finally to be with him – Philemon 1: 23

*The contradictions implicit in the Christian Gospel.* If the Gospels are read dispassionately and without prejudice, many examples of contradiction or inconsistency are to be found. Over and over again, the point is made that those who follow Christ will be rewarded in the afterlife, while those who do not will be banished from the kingdom of God and punished eternally. While Christians like to propagate their religion as one that is loving and merciful, such love and mercy is not available to all because, as Christ remarked, 'Many are called but few are chosen' – while on the other hand, 'As in Adam all die, so in Christ shall all be made alive.' Which text is correct? Answer: the one you would *like* to be correct, or the one which fits in best to the sermon you happen to be preaching.

There is a dark side to the message of Jesus Christ, which the compilers of the new Testament might have been better advised to delete:

*Jesus the family breaker.* Luke 12: 51-53:

> Suppose ye that I am come to give peace on earth? I tell you Nay; but rather division: For from henceforth there shall be five in one house divided, three against two and two against three. The father shall be divided against the son and the son against the father; the mother against the daughter and the daughter against the mother; the mother in law against the daughter in law and the daughter in law against her mother in law.

*Jesus the prophet of doom:* Luke 10, 10-18:

> But into whatsoever city ye enter, and they receive you not, go your ways out into the streets of the same, and say, 'Even the very dust of your city, which cleaveth on us, we do wipe off against you: notwithstanding be ye sure of this, that the kingdom of God is come nigh unto you.' But I say unto you, that it shall be more tolerable in that day for Sodom, than for that city. Woe unto thee, Chorazin! woe unto thee, Bethsaida! For if the mighty works had been done in Tyre and Sidon, which have been done in you, they had a great while ago repented, sitting in sackcloth and ashes. But it shall be more tolerable for Tyre and Sidon at the

judgment, than for you. And thou, Capernaum, which art exalted to Heaven, shalt be thrust down to Hell. He that heareth you heareth me; and he that despiseth you despiseth me; and he that despiseth me despiseth him that sent me.

*Jesus the anti–intellectual advocate of imprudence.* Luke 10: 19-21:

> Behold, I give unto you power to tread on serpents and scorpions, and over all the power of the enemy: and nothing shall by any means hurt you. Notwithstanding in this rejoice not, that the spirits are subject unto you; but rather rejoice, because your names are written in heaven. In that hour Jesus rejoiced in spirit, and said, I thank thee, O Father, Lord of heaven and earth, that thou hast hid these things from the wise and prudent, and hast revealed them unto babes: even so, Father; for so it seemed good in thy sight.

*Sceptical questions about the temptation in the wilderness.* In Luke 4: 1-15 we read:

> And Jesus being full of the Holy Ghost returned from Jordan, and was led by the Spirit into the wilderness, being forty days tempted of the devil. And in those days he did eat nothing: and when they were ended, he afterward hungered. And the devil said unto him, If thou be the Son of God, command this stone that it be made bread. And Jesus answered him, saying, It is written, That man shall not live by bread alone, but

by every word of God. And the devil, taking him up into an high mountain, shewed unto him all the kingdoms of the world in a moment of time. And the devil said unto him, All this power will I give thee, and the glory of them: for that is delivered unto me; and to whomsoever I will I give it. If thou therefore wilt worship me, all shall be thine. And Jesus answered and said unto him, Get thee behind me, Satan: for it is written, Thou shalt worship the Lord thy God, and him only shalt thou serve. And he brought him to Jerusalem, and set him on a pinnacle of the temple, and said unto him, If thou be the Son of God, cast thyself down from hence: For it is written, He shall give his angels charge over thee, to keep thee: And in their hands they shall bear thee up, lest at any time thou dash thy foot against a stone. And Jesus answering said unto him, It is said, Thou shalt not tempt the Lord thy God. And when the devil had ended all the temptation, he departed from him for a season. And Jesus returned in the power of the Spirit into Galilee: and there went out a fame of him through all the region round about. And he taught in their synagogues, being glorified of all.

This account does not really hold water. How do we know that Jesus ate nothing at all for forty days? What form did the devil take? Did Jesus go bodily up to a pinnacle on top of the temple in Jerusalem? If 'there went out a fame of him through all the region' who made this publicity possible? And, how did the story come into existence if it was not first told by Jesus himself?

Whether or not we interpret the episode as a metaphor for an inner mental struggle, the only way the author of the Gospel can have known about that struggle (assuming, of course, that he did not make the story up) must have been because Jesus chose to tell him about it. In doing so, Jesus appears to be guilty of self-pride – one of the sins he claims to have resisted in the wilderness.

In boasting about his close relationship to God and his ability to know the mind of God he set a precedent that encouraged religious leaders and statesmen to claim that they too have a direct line to God, and to indulge in similar self-glorification.

Today, anyone who came down from a mountain and said that he had successfully resisted temptation by the devil would be regarded as delusional – but perhaps he would find some who were sufficiently gullible to follow him and form a cult. That is what happened two thousand years ago, the only difference being that at that time people were far more superstitious and susceptible to arguments of persuasion. Belief in the possibility that a god could have a son was widespread, and because of the repressive domination of the world by Rome, whose emperor also claimed the title Son of God, there was a deep-felt need for a messiah or savior.

It seems extremely likely that the man Jesus saw this need, became convinced that he was that messiah, and set himself the task of challenging and subverting the authority of Rome in the most effective possible way, namely by claiming to be the son of God and, by offering himself as an eternal sacrifice, becoming the savior of mankind in the same sort of way as Prometheus.

*A possible solution to the puzzle.* Hearing voices and being subject to delusional imaginings of grandeur are symptoms of schizophrenia. If we look at the story of the temptation in the wilderness dispassionately, it seems on the face of it that Jesus might well have been schizophrenic. He certainly had all the symptoms. He believed himself to be the son of God, reportedly carried on a conversation with Satan, and believed that he could come to life again after death. He told his disciples that unless they ate his flesh and drank his blood they would not see the kingdom of God – but at the same time threatened that: 'whosoever shall eat this bread, and drink this cup of the Lord, unworthily, shall be guilty of the body and blood of the Lord. [...] For he that eateth and drinketh unworthily, eateth and drinketh damnation to himself [...]' (I Cor. 11: 27-29). He spoke of God as his personal father, and spoke of destroying the temple in Jerusalem. These wild claims are still believed by Christians, and they believe that they too can, through Jesus Christ, communicate with the godhead.

Is Christianity nothing more than a form of institutionalized schizophrenia? Is it a mental illness? A neurosis?

*Satan's hypothetical imperatives.* In challenging Jesus to jump off a pinnacle of the temple, Satan uses hypothetical imperatives to test three propositions, (i) that the quoted prophecy is reliable (ii) that Jesus' claim to be the son of God is valid, and (iii) that Jesus has the faith to prove that he is the son of God. Jesus fails on all three counts. The replies he makes are not so much answers as excuses: they are quite unconvincing and lacking in substance. All he can do is quote Scripture in the manner of a theologian or Bible scholar. If he really believed that he was the son of God and that God had given his angels charge over him, why did he not prove the truth of the prophecy by making a genuine leap of faith and jumping off the top of the temple?

We can only conclude from this account that Jesus could not have believed that the prophecy he quoted was entirely reliable, that he was only pretending to be the son of God, and that he knew very well that if he jumped off that pinnacle, he would jump to his death.

*Socrates and the immortality of the soul.* The Christian religion owes much to Socrates, for it was he who pointed out the absurdity of believing in gods who behaved badly, argued cogently for the immortality of the soul, and who went to his death willingly and cheerfully after being offered the opportunity to escape from Athens to a life of ease in the Greek equivalent of the Bahamas.

Nietzsche referred to Socratic philosophy as 'the birth of tragedy' because it opposed the free-thinking, risk-taking, creative spirit of Dionysus and replaced it with what he called 'Socratism', the cringing, underdog mentality that goes hand in hand with an obsession with the afterlife and fear of what may come after death. It is this obsession and this fear that provides the psychological basis upon which the Christian message stands. Take away the fear of death and hell, and the Gospel falls apart.

*The Socratic obsession.* Socrates' attitude to soul-immortality and life after death is well stated in this passage from the *Phaedo*:

> But then, O my friends, he said, if the soul is really immortal, what care should be taken of her, not only in respect of the portion of time which is called life, but of eternity! And the danger of neglecting her from

this point of view does indeed appear to be awful. If death had only been the end of all, the wicked would have had a good bargain in dying, for they would have been happily quit not only of their body, but of their own evil together with their souls. But now, inasmuch as the soul is manifestly immortal, there is no release or salvation from evil except the attainment of the highest virtue and wisdom. For the soul when on her progress to the world below takes nothing with her but nurture and education; and these are said greatly to benefit or greatly to injure the departed, at the very beginning of his journey thither.

Jesus used the Socratic obsession with the afterlife to brilliant effect. First, he claimed to be the son of God; second he offered himself as an eternal sacrifice for the salvation of souls and, lastly, he organized matters so that people believed in the resurrection of the dead and day of judgment when the good would be rewarded with heaven, and the bad cast down to hell.

Two hundred years later, when the spread of Christianity seemed unstoppable, such dire warnings suited the purpose of the administrators of the Roman Empire very well, as they served to keep the masses under discipline. It was no longer enough to strive for the attainment of the highest virtue and wisdom as had been the case when stoicism was the state philosophy. Now, much more was needed: strict conformity to rules, dogma and beliefs laid down by the new religious hierarchy of the Roman Empire.

Because the Church depended on the state and the state on the Church, both Church and state became increasingly authoritarian, so that religious disobedience was turned into a crime – in exactly the same way that crime and impiety were seen as identical in Athens five hundred years before. Thus was the clock put back, or at least stopped. At a time when geometers, mathematicians and natural philosophers were on the brink of a new leap forward in scientific knowledge, the Roman Catholic Church put a stop to that leap, and held science back until the Renaissance of the 16th century.

*The Myth of Er: 'a story worth telling'.* At the end of Plato's *Republic* Socrates tells the story of a man (Er) who comes back to life after being believed to have been killed in battle, and who has witnessed a Day of Judgment when new incarnations are allotted to the souls of the dead. Rather surprisingly for one who has made it his life's work to search for truth and justice and to attack the arguments of persuasion of sophists and rhetoricians, Socrates admits that although the story of Er may not be true, it is nevertheless worth telling, presumably because it will encourage piety and obedience to the state:

> When Er and the spirits arrived, their duty was to go at once to Lachesis; but first of all there came a prophet who arranged them in order; then he took from the knees of Lachesis lots and samples of lives, and having mounted a high pulpit, spoke as follows: 'Hear the word of Lachesis, the daughter of Necessity. Mortal souls, behold a new cycle of life and mortality. Your genius will not be allotted to you, but you choose your genius; and let him who draws the first lot have the first choice, and the life which he chooses shall be his destiny. Virtue is free, and as a man honors or dishonors her he will have

more or less of her; the responsibility is with the chooser – God is justified.' When the Interpreter had thus spoken he scattered lots indifferently among them all, and each of them took up the lot which fell near him, all but Er himself (he was not allowed), and each as he took his lot perceived the number which he had obtained. Then the Interpreter placed on the ground before them the samples of lives; and there were many more lives than the souls present, and they were of all sorts. There were lives of every animal and of man in every condition. And there were tyrannies among them, some lasting out the tyrant's life, others which broke off in the middle and came to an end in poverty and exile and beggary; and there were lives of famous men, some who were famous for their form and beauty as well as for their strength and success in games, or, again, for their birth and the qualities of their ancestors; and some who were the reverse of famous for the opposite qualities. And of women likewise; there was not, however, any definite character for them, because the soul, when choosing a new life, must of necessity become different. But there was every other quality, and all mingled with one another, and also with elements of wealth and poverty, and disease and health; and there were mean states also.

And here, my dear Glaucon, is the supreme peril of our human state; and therefore the utmost care should be taken. Let each one of us leave every other kind of knowledge and seek and follow one thing only, if peradventure he may be able to learn and may find someone who will make him able to learn and discern between good and evil, and so to choose always and everywhere the better life as he has opportunity. He should consider the bearing of all these things which have been mentioned severally and collectively upon virtue; he should know what the effect of beauty is when combined with poverty or wealth in a particular soul, and what are the good and evil consequences of noble and humble birth, of private and public station, of strength and weakness, of cleverness and dullness, and of all the soul, and the operation of them when conjoined; he will then look at the nature of the soul, and from the consideration of all these qualities he will be able to determine which is the better and which is the worse; and so he will choose, giving the name of evil to the life which will make his soul more unjust, and good to the life which will make his soul more just; all else he will disregard. For we have seen and know that this is the best choice both in life and after death. A man must take with him into the world below an adamantine faith in truth and right, that there too he may be undazzled by the desire of wealth or the other allurements of evil, lest, coming upon tyrannies and similar villainies, he do irremediable wrongs to others and suffer yet worse himself; but let him know how to choose the mean and avoid the extremes on either side, as far as possible, not only in this life but in all that which is to come. For this is the way of happiness.

And according to the report of the messenger from the other world this was what the prophet said at the time: 'Even for the last comer, if he chooses wisely and will live diligently, there is appointed a happy and not undesirable existence. Let not him who chooses first be careless, and let not the last despair.' And when he had spoken, he who had the first choice came forward and in a moment chose the greatest tyranny; his mind having been darkened by folly and sensuality, he had not thought out the whole matter before he chose, and did not at first sight perceive that he was fated, among other evils, to devour his own children. But when he had time to reflect, and saw what was in the lot, he began to beat his breast and lament over his choice, forgetting the proclamation of the prophet; for, instead of throwing the blame of his misfortune on himself, he accused chance and the gods, and everything rather than himself. Now he was one of those who came from heaven and in a former life had dwelt in a well-ordered state, but his virtue was a matter of habit only, and he had no philosophy. And it was true of others who were similarly overtaken, that the greater number of them came from heaven and therefore they had never been schooled by trial, whereas the pilgrims who came from earth, having themselves suffered and seen others suffer, were not in a hurry to choose. And owing to this inexperience of theirs, and also because the lot was a chance, many of the souls exchanged a good destiny for an evil or an evil for a good. For if a man had always on his arrival in this world dedicated himself from the first to sound philosophy, and had been moderately fortunate in the number of the lot, he might, as the messenger reported, be happy here, and also his journey to another life and return to this, instead of being rough and underground, would be smooth and heavenly. Most curious, he said, was the spectacle – sad and laughable and strange; for the choice of the souls was in most cases based on their experience of a previous life. There he saw the soul which had once been Orpheus choosing the life of a swan out of enmity to the race of women, hating to be born of a woman because they had been his murderers; he beheld also the soul of Thamyras choosing the life of a nightingale; birds, on the other hand, like the swan and other musicians, wanting to be men. The soul which obtained the twentieth lot chose the life of a lion, and this was the soul of Ajax the son of Telamon, who would not be a man, remembering the injustice which was done him in the judgment about the arms. The next was Agamemnon, who took the life of an eagle, because, like Ajax, he hated human nature by reason of his sufferings. About the middle came the lot of Atalanta; she, seeing the great fame of an athlete, was unable to resist the temptation: and after her there followed the soul of Epeus the son of Panopeus passing into the nature of a woman cunning in the arts; and far away among the last who chose, the soul of the jester Thersites was putting on the form of a monkey.

There came also the soul of Odysseus having yet to make a choice, and his lot happened to be the last of them all. Now the recollection of former tolls had disenchanted him of ambition, and he went about for a considerable time in search of the life of a private man who had no cares; he had some difficulty in finding this, which was lying about and had been neglected by everybody else; and when he saw it, he said that he would have done the same had his lot been first instead of last, and that he was delighted to have it. And not only did men pass into animals, but I must also mention that there were animals tame and wild who changed into one another and into corresponding human natures – the good into the gentle and the evil into the savage, in all sorts of combinations.

And thus, Glaucon, the tale has been saved and has not perished, and will save us if we are obedient to the word spoken; and we shall pass safely over the river of Forgetfulness and our soul will not be defiled. Wherefore my counsel is that we hold fast ever to the heavenly way and follow after justice and virtue always, considering that the soul is immortal and able to endure every sort of good and every sort of evil. Thus shall we live dear to one another and to the gods, both while remaining here and when, like conquerors in the games who go round to gather gifts, we receive our reward. And it shall be well with us both in this life and in the pilgrimage of a thousand years which we have been describing.

Notice the similarity between the story of Odysseus being the last to choose and being happy with his choice with the words of Jesus: 'For the first shall be last, and the last first.'

We do not know what Jesus did between the ages of twelve and thirty-three, but judging from his knowledge of Scripture and his sayings, it seems likely that he must have made a study of philosophy, particularly Platonic philosophy. This, coupled with shrewd political insight, enabled him to construct his own life story in such a way as to bring down the authority of Rome, which as a Jew of proven descent from the royal House of David must surely have been his principal objective.

*The Christian myth of the Last Judgment.* Compared with The Myth of Er, the last judgment as described in the Book of Revelation in the New Testament contains a far more frightening and unjust threat for evil doers and non-Christians. While Socrates holds out the hope that evil doers may be able to mend their ways in a later incarnation, no such hope is available to those who do not accept Christ or believe in the Christian gospel.

Read with an open mind, the following passage from the Book of Revelation appears not merely ridiculous but malevolent and nasty. Only a little child, a gullible fool or a coward could be taken in by such nonsense:

> And I saw an angel come down from heaven, having the key of the bottomless pit and a great chain in his hand. And he laid hold on the dragon, that old serpent, which is the Devil, and Satan, and bound him a thousand years, and cast him into the bottomless pit, and shut him up, and set a seal upon him, that he should deceive the na-

tions no more, till the thousand years should be fulfilled: and after that he must be loosed a little season. And I saw thrones, and they sat upon them, and judgment was given unto them: and I saw the souls of them that were beheaded for the witness of Jesus, and for the word of God, and which had not worshipped the beast, neither his image, neither had received his mark upon their foreheads, or in their hands; and they lived and reigned with Christ a thousand years. But the rest of the dead lived not again until the thousand years were finished. This is the first resurrection. Blessed and holy is he that hath part in the first resurrection: on such the second death hath no power, but they shall be priests of God and of Christ, and shall reign with him a thousand years. And when the thousand years are expired, Satan shall be loosed out of his prison, and shall go out to deceive the nations which are in the four quarters of the earth, Gog and Magog, to gather them together to battle: the number of whom is as the sand of the sea. And they went up on the breadth of the earth, and compassed the camp of the saints about, and the beloved city: and fire came down from God out of heaven, and devoured them. And the devil that deceived them was cast into the lake of fire and brimstone, where the beast and the false prophet are, and shall be tormented day and night for ever and ever. And I saw a great white throne, and him that sat on it, from whose face the earth and the heaven fled away; and there was found no place for them. And I saw the dead, small and great, stand before God; and the books were opened: and another book was opened, which is the book of life: and the dead were judged out of those things which were written in the books, according to their works. And the sea gave up the dead which were in it; and death and hell delivered up the dead which were in them: and they were judged every man according to their works. And death and hell were cast into the lake of fire. This is the second death. And whosoever was not found written in the book of life was cast into the lake of fire.

Book of Revelation, Chapter 20

Take away the fear of eternal punishment, replace it with the certainty that we are all one and that on death the individual mind is reabsorbed into the infinite and eternal mind, and the whole Christian edifice of guilt, sin and eternal punishment collapses like a house of cards.

*Why should we believe the Bible?* Because the Bible is a collection of books rather than a single book by a single author, belief in the Bible can only be based on further beliefs: first, that the correct books were included; second, that no books were excluded that should have been included; and third, that no books were included that should have been excluded.

We also have to believe that the text of every book in the Bible was both accurately translated and accurately transcribed. To believe otherwise would be to believe that the inspired word of God contained mistakes.

Because there are many translations which vary in detail, there are equally many hermeneutical interpretations of those translations. There is a world of difference, for instance, between the King James Version: 'Peace and good will to all men' and the Douai version: 'Peace to men of good will'. Again, Roman Catholics believe that when Jesus said 'Upon this rock I will build my church' he was referring to Peter; while Protestants believe that the rock he referred to was Peter's affirmation that Jesus was 'the Christ, the son of the living God'. While Roman Catholics believe that bread and wine are actually turned into the body and blood of Christ during the Mass, Protestants believe that the bread and wine are symbols of the body and blood, and that the act of eating and drinking is a symbolic celebration rather than a real re-enactment. How are we to know which opinion to believe or which translation to trust? This is a question theologians prefer not to address. Instead, they claim that the Bible is the inspired word of God, and as such must be true; and that texts that appear to be historically contradictory or empirically impossible appear to be so not because they really are contradictory or impossible, but because someone else's interpretation of them is incorrect or someone else's understanding is inadequate. However, theologians, preachers and religious people seldom, if ever, admit that they might be wrong.

The Roman Catholic Church even goes so far as to turn doubt into a sin. In this way they suffocate reason, outlaw scepticism and encourage the faithful to adopt an anti-intellectual mindset.

*Hermeneutical interpretation.* We are connected, however distantly, to every text we read. Reader and text are like two ships, each hull down on the horizon of the other. They sail on the same sea of understanding and their horizons overlap. In making a serious study of a text we have to enter into a hermeneutical negotiation with it in which the epistemic horizon of the reader is enlarged by the text, and the text's horizon is enlarged by the reader. However great the distance in time or culture between author and reader, shared humanity always provides an overlap of horizons, and it is this overlap that makes it possible to understand a text and bring new understanding to it. The process of coming to a fuller understanding of a text is one of extending and enlarging that overlap, and is achieved by conducting a conversation with the text in which questions are posed by the reader of the text and by the text of the reader. So the hermeneutical process is circular, or recursive, like a game whose rules one learns by playing it.

Language can be viewed as a continuous web or structure in which words act as centers of force and provide a holistic picture of a past world and the moods that prevailed within it. The mood, language and horizon of every world overlap. Each extends outwards to infinity and is connected to every other, however tenuously. Because every text stands open to and is enriched by each new comprehension, there can be no fixed, dogmatic or canonical interpretation of any text that purports to reveal the word of God.

*Innner infinity of a text.* Human understanding is a process whereby horizons are fused and their overlap is extended. Like the lens of a telescope through which a distant object is viewed by an observer, language is the medium of understanding that lies between a text and its reader. Anyone who seriously and rationally seeks to understand what is said or written is drawn into an infinity of what is unsaid or unwritten, so that every conversation with a text has its own inner infinity, and any absolute distinction between horizons or between the past and the present must be rejected.

*Spinoza's critical analysis.* Displaying great philosophical and political courage, Spinoza applied his mind to the question of the interpretation of Scripture. His excellent knowledge of languages gave him an unparalleled linguistic access to virtually all the latest works of Hebraic and Christian philosophy, and enabled him to make what is probably the most unprejudiced critical analysis of the Bible ever written.

\* \* \*

## Extracts from Spinoza's
## *Theologico-Political Treatise*

(Where appropriate, the name 'God' has been replaced by 'Iota' and 'Divine' by 'Iotic' in this section)

We need no longer scruple to affirm that the prophets only perceived God's revelation by the aid of imagination, that is, by words and figures either real or imaginary. We find no other means mentioned in Scripture, and therefore must not invent any. As to the particular law of Nature by which the communications took place, I confess my ignorance. I might, indeed, say as others do, that they took place by the power of God; but this would be mere trifling, and no better than explaining some unique specimen by a transcendental term. Everything takes place by the power of God. Nature herself is the power of God under another name, and ignorance of the power of God is co-extensive with our ignorance of Nature. It is absolute folly, therefore, to ascribe an event to the power of God when we know not its natural cause, which is the power of God.

Since the power in Nature is identical with the power of God, by which alone all things happen and are determined, it follows that whatsoever man, as a part of Nature, provides himself with to aid and preserve his existence, or whatsoever Nature affords him without his help, is given to him solely by the Divine power, acting either through human nature or through external circumstances. So whatever human nature can furnish itself with by its own efforts to preserve its existence may be fitly called the inward aid of God, whereas whatever else accrues to man's profit from outward causes may be called the external aid of God.

We can now easily understand what is meant by the election of God. For since no one can do anything save by the predetermined order of Nature, that is by God's eternal ordinance and decree, it follows that no one can choose a plan of life for himself, or accomplish any work save by God's vocation choosing him for the work or the plan of life in question, rather than any other. Lastly, by fortune, I mean the ordinance of God insofar as it directs human life through external and unexpected means.

Law then, being a plan of living which men have a certain object laid down to themselves or others may, as it seems, be divided into human law and Iotic law.

By human law, I mean a plan of living which serves only to render life and the state secure. By Iotic law, I mean that which only regards the highest good, in other words, the true knowledge of Iota and love.

[...] Since without Iota nothing can exist or be conceived, it is evident that all natural phenomena involve and express the conception of Iota as far as their essence and perfection extend, so that we have greater and more perfect knowledge of Iota in proportion to our knowledge of natural phenomena; conversely, the greater our knowledge of natural phenomena, the more perfect is our knowledge of the essence of Iota. So then, our highest good not only depends on the knowledge of Iota, but wholly consists therein; and it further follows that a man is perfect or the reverse in proportion to the nature and perfection of the object of his special desire: hence the most perfect and the chief sharer in the highest blessedness is he who prizes above all else and takes a special delight in the intellectual knowledge of Iota, the most perfect being.

As the love of Iota is man's highest happiness and blessedness, and the ultimate end and aim of all human actions, it follows that he alone lives by the Iotic law who loves Iota, not from fear of punishment, or from love of any other object such as sensual pleasure, fame, or the like; but simply because he has knowledge of Iota, or is convinced that the knowledge and love of Iota is the highest good. The sum and chief precept, then, of the Iotic law is to love Iota as the highest good, namely, as we have said, not from fear of any pains and penalties, or from the love of any other object in which we desire to take pleasure. The idea of Iota lays down the rule that Iota is our highest good – in other words, that the knowledge and love of Iota is the ultimate aim, to which all action should be directed. The worldling cannot understand these things, they appear foolishness to him, because he has too meagre a knowledge of Iota, and also because in this highest good he can discover nothing which he can handle or eat, or which affects the fleshly appetites wherein he chiefly delights, for it consists only in thought and pure reason. They, on the other hand, who know that they possess no greater gift than intellect and sound reason, will doubtless accept what I have said without question.

If we consider the nature of Iotic law, as we have just explained it, we shall see:

    I. That it is universal or common to all men, for we have deduced it from universal human nature.
    II. That it does not depend on the truth of any historical narrative whatsoever, for inasmuch as the Iotic law is comprehended solely by the consideration of human nature, and it is plain that we can conceive it as existing as well in Adam as in any other man, as well in a man living among his fellows, as in the man who lives by himself.

We have seen that he who acts rightly from the true knowledge and love of right acts with freedom and constancy, whereas he who acts from fear of evil is under the constraint of evil and acts in bondage and external control.

The Iotic law, which renders men truly blessed, and teaches them the true life, is universal to all men; nay, we have so intimately deduced it from human nature that it must be esteemed innate, and, as it were, ingrained in the human mind.

When people declare, as they are all ready to do, that the Bible is the word of God teaching man true blessedness and the way of salvation, they evidently do not mean what they say; the masses take no pains at all to live according to Scripture, and we see most people endeavouring to hawk about their own commentaries as the word of God, and giving their best efforts, under the guise of religion, to compelling others to think as they do: we generally see, I say, theologians anxious to learn how to wring their inventions and sayings out of the most sacred text, and to fortify them with Divine authority. Such persons never display less scruple or more zeal than when they are interpreting Scripture or the mind of the Holy Ghost; if we ever see them perturbed, it is not that they fear to attribute some error to the Holy Spirit, and to stray from the right path, but that they are afraid to be convicted of error by others and thus to overthrow and bring into contempt their own authority.

Ambition and unscrupulousness have waxed so powerful, that religion is thought to consist, not so much in respecting the writings of the Holy Ghost, as in defending human commentaries, so that religion is no longer identified with charity, but with spreading discord and propagating insensate hatred, and is disguised under the name of a zeal for the Lord, and eager ardour.

To these evils we must add superstition, which teaches men to despise reason and nature, and only to admire and venerate that which is repugnant to both: whence it is not wonderful that for the sake of increasing the admiration and veneration felt for Scripture, men strive to explain it so as to make it appear to contradict, as far as possible, both one and the other: thus they dream that the most profound mysteries lie hid in the Bible, and weary themselves out in the investigation of these absurdities, to the neglect of what is useful. Every result of their diseased imagination they attribute to the Holy Ghost, and strive to defend with the utmost zeal and passion: for it is an observed fact that men employ their reason to defend conclusions arrived at by reason, but conclusions arrived at by the passions are defended by the passions.

If we would separate ourselves from the crowd and escape from theological prejudices, instead of rashly accepting human commentaries for Divine documents, we must consider the true method of interpreting Scripture and dwell upon it at some length: for if we remain in ignorance of this we cannot know, certainly, what the Bible and the Holy Spirit wish to teach. I may sum up the matter by saying that the method of interpreting Scripture does not differ widely from the method of interpreting Nature – in fact, it is almost the same. For as the interpretation of Nature consists in the examination of the history of Nature, and therefore deducing definitions of natural phenomena on certain fixed axioms, so Scriptural interpretation proceeds by the examination of Scripture, and inferring the intention of its authors as a legitimate conclusion from its fundamental principles.

I remember once to have read in some book that a man named Orlando Furioso used to drive a kind of winged monster through the air, fly over any countries he liked, kill unaided vast numbers of men and giants and suchlike fancies, which from the point of view of reason are obviously absurd. A very similar story I read in Ovid of Perseus, and also in the books of Judges and Kings of Samson, who alone and unarmed killed thousands of men, and of Elijah, who flew through the air, and at last went up to heaven in a chariot of fire, with horses of fire. All these stories are obviously alike, but we judge them very differently. The first only sought to amuse, the second had a political object, the third a religious object. We gather this simply from the opinions we had previously formed of the authors. But it is evidently necessary to know something of the authors of writings which are obscure or unintelligible, if we would interpret their meaning; and for the same reason, in order to choose a proper reading from a man of great variety, we ought to have information as to the versions in which the differences are found, and as to the possibility of other readings having been discovered by persons of greater authority.

[...] the difficulty of interpreting Scripture arises from no defect in human reason, but simply from the callousness (not to say malice) of men who neglected the history of the Bible, while there were still materials for enquiry; secondly, from the fact (admitted, I think, by all) that the supernatural faculty is a divine gift granted only to the faithful. But the prophets and apostles did not preach to the faithful only, but chiefly to the unfaithful and wicked. Such persons, therefore, were able to understand the intention of the prophets and apostles, otherwise the prophets and apostles would have seemed to be preaching to little boys and infants, not to men endowed with reason. Moses, too, would have given his laws in vain, if they could only be comprehended by the faithful, who need no law. Indeed, those who demand supernatural faculties for comprehending the meaning of the prophets and apostles seem truly lacking in natural faculties, so that we should hardly suppose such persons the possessors of the Divine supernatural gift.

As to the tradition of the Pharisees, we have already shown that it is not consistent, while the authority of the popes of Rome stands in need of more credible evidence; the latter, indeed, I reject simply on this ground, for if the popes could point out to us the meaning of Scripture as surely as did the high priests of the Jews, I should not be deterred by the fact that there have been heretic and impious Roman pontiffs; for among the Jewish high priests of old there were also heretics and impious men who gained the high priesthood by improper means, but who, nevertheless, had scriptural sanction for their supreme power of interpreting the law.

However, as the popes can show no such sanction, their authority remains open to very grave doubt, nor should anyone be deceived by the example of the Jewish high priests and think that the Catholic religion also stands in need of a pontiff; he should bear in mind that the laws of Moses being also the ordinary laws of the country, necessarily required some public authority to ensure their observance; for, if everyone were free to interpret the laws of his country as he pleased, no state could stand, but would for that very reason be dissolved at once, and public rights would become private rights.

With religion the case is widely different. Inasmuch as it consists not so much in outward actions as in simplicity and truth of character, it stands outside the sphere of law and public authority. Simplicity and truth of character are not produced by the constraint of laws, nor by the authority of the state, no one in the whole world over can be forced or legislated into a state of blessedness; the means required for such a consummation are faithful and brotherly admonition, sound education, and, above all, free use of the individual judgment.

Therefore, as the supreme right of free thinking, even on religion, is in every man's power, and as it is inconceivable that such power could be alienated, it is also in every man's power to wield the supreme right and authority of free judgment in this behalf, and to explain and interpret religion for himself. The only reason for vesting the supreme authority in the interpretation of law, and judgment on public affairs in the hands of the magistrates, is that it concerns questions of public right. Similarly, the supreme authority in explaining religion, and in passing judgment thereon, is lodged with the individual, because it concerns questions of individual right. So far, then, from the authority of the Hebrew high priests telling in confirmation of the authority of the Roman pontiffs to interpret religion, it would rather tend to establish individual freedom of judgment. [...] For as the highest power of scriptural interpretation belongs to every man, the rule for such interpretation should be nothing but the natural light of reason, which is common to all – not any supernatural light nor any external authority; moreover, such a rule ought not to be so difficult that it can only be applied by very skilful philosophers, but should be adapted to the natural and ordinary faculties and capacity of mankind.

[...] the sacredness of Scripture depends on our understanding of the doctrines therein signified, and not on the words, the language, and the phrases in which these doctrines are conveyed to us; and it would further show us that books which teach and speak of whatever is highest and best are equally sacred, whatever be the tongue in which they are written, or the nation to which they belong.

If all the apostles had adopted the same method of teaching, and had all built up the Christian religion on the same foundation, Paul would have had no reason to call the work of a fellow apostle 'another man's foundation', inasmuch as it would have been identical with his own: his calling it another man's proved that each apostle built up his religious instruction on different foundations, thus resembling other teachers who have each their own method, and prefer instructing quite ignorant people who have never learnt enough under another master, whether the subject be science, languages, or even the indisputable truths of mathematics. Furthermore, if we go through the Epistles at all attentively, we shall see that the apostles, while agreeing about religion itself, are at variance as to the foundations it rests on. Paul, in order to strengthen men's religion, and show them that salvation depends only on the grace of God, teaches that no one can boast of works, but only of faith, and that no one can be justified by works (Romans 3: 27-28); in fact, he preaches the complete doctrine of predestination. James, on the other hand, states that man is justified by works, and not by faith only (see his Epistle, 2: 24), and omitting all the disputations of Paul, confines religion to a very few elements.

Religion was imparted to the early Hebrews as a law written down, because they were at that time in the condition of children, but afterwards, Moses (Deut. 30: 6) and Jeremiah (31: 33), predicted a time coming when the Lord should write his law in their hearts. Thus only the Jews, and amongst them chiefly the Sadducees, struggled for the law written on tablets; least of all need those who bear it inscribed on their hearts join in the contest.
    [...] Still, it will be said, though the law of God is written in the heart, the Bible is nonetheless the Word of God, and it is no more lawful to say of Scripture than of God's Word that it is mutilated and corrupted. I fear that such objectors are too anxious to be pious, and that they are in danger of turning religion into superstition, and worshiping paper and ink in place of God's Word.

Religion [...] consists, not in ceremonies, but in charity, and a true heart [...].

We can only judge a man faithful or unfaithful by his works. If his works be good, he is faithful, however much his doctrines may differ from those of the rest of the faithful: if his works be evil, though he may verbally conform, he is unfaithful. For obedience implies faith, and faith without works is dead.

[...] is a man to assent to anything against his reason? What is denial, if it be not reason's refusal to assent? In short, I am astonished that anyone should wish to subject reason, the greatest of gifts and a light from on high, to the dead letter which may have been corrupted by human malice; that it should be thought no crime to speak with contempt of mind, the true handwriting of God's word, calling it corrupt, blind, and lost, while it is considered the greatest of crimes to say the same of the letter, which is merely the reflection and image of God's word. Men think it pious to trust nothing to reason and their own judgment, and impious to doubt the faith of those who have transmitted to us the sacred books. Such conduct is not piety, but mere folly. And, after all, why are they so anxious? What are they afraid of? Do they think that faith and religion cannot be upheld unless men purposely keep themselves in ignorance, and turn their backs on reason? If this be so, they have but a timid trust in Scripture.

It is untrue that Scripture never contradicts itself directly, but only by implication. Moses says in so many words (Deuteronomy 4: 24), 'the Lord my God is a consuming fire' and elsewhere expressly denies that God has any likeness to visible things. If it be decided that the latter passage only contradicts the former by implication, and must be adapted thereto, lest it seemed to negate it, let us grant that God is a fire; or rather, lest we should seem to have taken leave of our senses, let us pass the matter over and take another example [...]. Samuel expressly denies that God ever repents, 'for he is not a man that he should repent' (1 Samuel xv. 29), Jeremiah, on the other hand, asserts that God does repent, both of the evil and of the good which he had intended to do (Jeremiah 18: 8-10). What? Are not these two texts directly contradictory? Which of the two, then, would the author want to explain metaphorically? Both statements are general, and each is the opposite of the other – what one flatly affirms, the other flatly denies.

The sphere of reason is, as we have said, truth and wisdom; the sphere of theology is piety and obedience. The power of reason does not extend so far as to determine for us that men may be blessed through simple obedience, without understanding. Theology tells us nothing else, enjoins on us no command save obedience, and has neither the will nor the power to oppose reason: she defines the dogmas of faith [...] only insofar as they may be necessary for obedience, and leaves reason to determine their precise truth: for reason is the light of the mind, and without her all things are dreams and phantoms. [...] To sum up, we may draw the absolute conclusion that the Bible must not be accommodated to reason, nor reason to the Bible.

* * *

*Spinoza's disagreement with Descartes.* Aristotle defined substance as 'that which depends on no other thing for its existence'. In his *Principles of Philosophy*

(Section 51), Descartes takes Aristotle's definition to be axiomatic, pointing out that, on the basis of substance depending on no other thing for its existence, there can be only one substance – the infinite substance that we call God. But he then goes on to transgress his own axiom, introducing two more substances, mind and matter – both of which rely for their existence upon God.

Spinoza saw the inconsistency of Descartes' argument and, returning to Aristotle's original definition, argued in Euclidean style from basic axioms for a single, infinite substance (*Deus-sive-Natura*, 'God, which is to say Nature') conceived under infinite attributes, what appear to us as individual things being modes of that single substance rather than substances in their own right.

*The Cartesian circle.* Descartes believed that his Cogito argument provided a rational demonstration of his own and God's existence, and how human knowledge is possible, claiming that all his ideas that were clear and distinct were certain knowledge and guaranteed by God. His argument presupposes substance dualism, and is obviously circular. It goes as follows:

   1. I doubt my existence.
   2. Every time I doubt, I think.
   3. I think, therefore I am a thinking thing.
   4. I am a thinking thing, therefore I am, I exist.
   5. Because the idea I have of my own existence is clear and distinct, all my ideas that are clear and distinct must be productive of certainty.
   6. I have a clear and distinct idea of the existence of God, therefore God exists.

7. As a perfect and supreme being, God does not deceive.

8. Because God does not deceive, all my ideas that are clear and distinct (including the validity of this argument) are guaranteed by Him.

This argument can be reduced to 'every time I doubt my existence I can be certain of my existence', which can be further reduced to 'if doubt then no doubt' or 'if p then not p' – a logical contradiction. Also, when Descartes claims that because his clear and distinct idea of God has yielded certainty this once, *all* his other clear and distinct ideas will also yield certainty, he is arguing from the particular to the general.

The cause of the confusion is substance dualism. Descartes is unable to relinquish his presupposition that God and Nature are separate, or that mind and matter are separate. Spinoza used rigorous argument to resolve the Cartesian confusion in his masterpiece, *Ethics*.

\* \* \*

## Extracts from Spinoza's *Ethics*
(In this section 'God' is replaced by 'Iota' and 'Divine' by 'Iotic')

Part I: Of Iota

Definitions:

1: By cause of itself, I understand that whose essence involves existence, or that whose nature cannot be conceived except as existing.

2: That thing is said to be finite in its own kind that can be limited by another of the same nature. For example, the body is called finite because we always conceive another that is greater. Thus a thought is limited by another thought, but the body is not limited by thought nor thought by body.

3: By substance, I understand what is in itself and is conceived through itself, that is, that whose concept does not require the concept of another thing, from which it must be formed.

[Later, Spinoza will show that there can be only one substance, Iota.]

4: By attribute, I understand what the intellect perceives of a substance, as constituting its essence.

5: By mode, I understand the affections of a substance, or that which is in another through which it is also conceived.

[A 'mode' is a 'way of being'. Necessarily, Iota is conceived not only under infinite attributes, but under infinite modes of those attributes.]

6: By Iota, I understand a being absolutely infinite, that is, a substance consisting of an infinity of attributes, of which each one expresses an eternal and infinite essence.

[A being that is absolutely infinite is infinitely inclusive. Nothing can exist 'outside' it, because there is no outside. This axiom excludes the possibility of the existence of a God that is said to stand outside Nature.]

7: The thing is called free which exists from the necessity of its nature alone, and is determined to act by itself alone. But a thing is called necessary, or rather compelled, which is determined by another to exist and to produce an effect in a certain and determinate manner.

[Only Iota exists from the necessity of its nature alone, so, as we shall see, only Iota is free. Because we are finite modes of Iota, we share, to a very limited extent, in Iota's freedom.]

8: By eternity, I understand existence itself, insofar as it is conceived to follow necessarily from the definition alone of the eternal thing. [...] For such existence, like the essence of the thing, is conceived as an eternal truth, and on that account cannot be explained by duration or time, even if the duration is conceived to be without beginning or end.

[Spinoza's rejection of the concept of duration or time as an explanation of existence anticipates presentism, the view that the past, present and the future are not separate, and that every event – even cosmic events like the supposed big bang or big crunch – can only be legitimately expressed as taking place in the present.]

Propositions:

1. A substance is prior in nature to its affections.

[The meaning of 'affections' (*affectiones*) is difficult to define. Some translations have 'modifications'.]

2. Substances having different attributes have nothing in common with one another.

[This proposition prepares the ground for propositions 13 and 14, which show that there can be only one substance, Iota.]

3. If things have nothing in common with one another, one of them cannot be the cause of the other.

[From a theological point of view, acceptance of this proposition necessitates acceptance of the proposition that God and Nature must have something in common.]

4. Two or more distinct things are distinguished from one another either by a difference in the attributes of the substance or by a difference in their affections.

5. In nature there cannot be two or more substances of the same nature or attribute.

[This proposition rules out the possibility of parallel universes or a 'multiverse'.]

6. One substance cannot be produced by another substance.

7. It pertains to the nature of a substance to exist.

8. Every substance is necessarily infinite.

9. The more reality or being each thing has, the more attributes belong to it.

[So an infinite being must have infinite attributes]

10. Each attribute of a substance must be conceived through itself.

11. Iota, or a substance consisting of infinite attributes, each of which expresses eternal and infinite essence, necessarily exists.

12. No attribute of a substance can be truly conceived from which it follows that the substance can be divided.

13. A substance which is absolutely infinite is indivisible.

14. Except Iota, no substance can be or be conceived.

15. Whatever is, is in Iota, and nothing can be or be conceived without Iota.

16. From the necessity of the Iotic nature, there must follow infinitely many things in infinitely many modes, (i.e., everything which can fall under an infinite intellect).

17. Iota acts from the laws of its nature alone, and is compelled by no one.

[Here we can see what arrogance it is to suppose that we have what we call 'free will', for, as modes of thought and matter, we are compelled to act from the laws of Nature.]

18. Iota is the immanent, not the transitive, cause of all things.

[This proposition forms the basis for Hegel's *Zeitgeist*, the difference between Hegel and Spinoza being that Hegel confers a teleological element to *Zeitgeist*, suggesting that it drives the universe onwards and upwards towards an ideal state.]

19. Iota is eternal, or, all Iota's attributes are eternal.

[This proposition denies the possibility of an absolute beginning or an absolute end: no absolute big bang, no absolute big crunch.]

20. Iota's existence and its essence are one and the same.

[The principal of existentialism]

21. All the things which follow from the absolute nature of any of Iota's attributes have always had to exist and be infinite, or are, through the same attribute, eternal and infinite.

29. In nature there is nothing contingent, but all things are determined from the necessity of the Iotic nature to exist and produce an effect in a certain way.

Scholium: Before I proceed further, I wish to explain here – or rather to advise the reader – what we must understand by *Natura naturans* and *Natura naturata*. For from the preceding I think it is already established that by *Natura naturans* we must understand what is in itself and is conceived through itself, or such attributes of substance as express an eternal and infinite essence, that is, Iota insofar as it is considered as a free cause. But by *Natura naturata*, I understand whatever follows from the necessity of Iota's nature, or from any of Iota's attributes, that is, all the modes of Iota's attributes insofar as they are considered as things which are in Iota, and can neither be nor be conceived without Iota.

[*Natura naturans* and *Natura naturata* are two of the attributes of Iota and correspond roughly to Schopenhauer's Will and Representation. The same sort of concept is expressed by Einstein's equation $E = mc^2$.]

30. An actual intellect, whether finite or infinite, must comprehend Iota's attributes and Iota's affections, and nothing else.

31. The actual intellect, whether finite or infinite, like will, desire, love, and the like, must be referred to *Natura Naturata* not to *Natura naturans*.

32. The will cannot be called a free cause, but only a necessary one.

[Perhaps the most contentious of all Spinoza's propositions. We do not have free will; but we feel, as Sartre puts it, 'condemned' to act as if we do have it. Frank Sinatra may have *believed* that he did it his way, but in fact he was only able to do it in the way that he did.]

33. Things could have been produced by Iota in no other way, and in no other order than they have been produced.

[This proposition does away with the possibility of speaking rationally about counterfactual worlds.]

34. Iota's power is its essence itself.

Demonstration: For from the necessity alone of Iota's essence, it follows that Iota is the cause of itself and of all things. Therefore, Iota's power, by which it and all things are and act, is its essence in itself.

[Once again, Spinoza shows the logical impossibility of the existence of a creator or designer God who stands 'outside' Nature.]

36. Nothing exists from whose nature some effect does not follow.

Demonstration: whatever exists expresses the nature, or essence of Iota in a certain and determinate way, that is, whatever exists expresses in a certain and determinate way the power of Iota, which is the cause of all things.

APPENDIX TO PART I

With these demonstrations, I have explained Iota's nature and properties: that it exists necessarily; that it is unique; that it is and acts from the necessity alone of its nature; that (and how) it is the free cause of all things; that all things are in Iota and so depend on it; that without it they can neither be nor be conceived; and finally, that all things have been predetermined by Iota, not from freedom of the will or absolute good pleasure, but from Iota's absolute nature, or infinite power.

Part II: OF THE MIND

7. The order and connection of ideas is the same as the order and connection of things.

Scholium: [...] Whatever can be perceived by an infinite intellect as constituting an essence of substance pertains to one substance only, and consequently the thinking substance and the extended substance are one and the same substance, which is now comprehended under this attribute, now under that. So also the mode of extension and the idea of that mode are one and the same thing, but expressed in two ways. Some of the Hebrews seem to have seen this as if through a cloud when they maintained that God, God's intellect, and the things understood by God are one and the same.

11. The first thing which constitutes the actual being of the human mind is nothing but the idea of a singular thing which actually exists.

Corollary: from this it follows that the human mind is a part of the infinite intellect of Iota. Therefore, when we say that the human mind perceives this or that, we are saying nothing but that Iota, not insofar as it is infinite, but insofar as it is explained through the nature of the human mind, or insofar as it constitutes the essence of the human mind, has this or that idea; and when we say that Iota has this or that idea, not only insofar as it constitutes the nature of the human mind, but insofar as it also has the idea of another thing together with the human mind, then we say that the human mind perceives the thing only partially, or inadequately.

13. The object of the idea constituting the human mind is the body, or a certain mode of extension which actually exists, and nothing else.

Scholium: From these propositions we understand not only that the human mind is united to the body, but also what should be understood by the union of mind and body. But no one will be able to understand it adequately, or distinctly, unless he first knows adequately the nature of our body. For the things we have shown so far are completely general and do not pertain more to man than to other individuals, all of which, though in different degrees, are nevertheless animate. For of each thing there is necessarily an idea in Iota, of which Iota is the cause in the same way as it is of the idea of the human body. And so, whatever we have said of the idea of the human body must also be said of the idea of any thing.

20. There is also in Iota an idea, or knowledge, of the human mind, which follows in Iota in the same way and is related to Iota in the same way as the idea, or knowledge, of the human body.

Demonstration: Thought is an attribute of Iota, and so there must necessarily be in Iota an idea both of thought and of all its affections, and consequently, of the human mind also.

21. This idea of the mind is united to the mind in the same way as the mind is united to the body.

26. The human mind does not perceive any external body as actually existing, except through the ideas of the affections of its own body.

[Note the similarity between Spinoza's 'ideas of the mind' and 'affections of the body' with Kant's 'concepts' and 'intuitions'.]

30. We can have only an entirely inadequate knowledge of the duration of our body.

Demonstration: Our body's duration depends neither on its essence nor even on Iota's absolute nature. But it is determined to exist and produce an effect from such other causes as are also determined by others to exist and produce an effect in a certain and determinate manner, and these again by others, and so to infinity. Therefore, the duration of our body depends on the common order of nature and the constitution of things. But adequate knowledge of how things are constituted is in Iota, insofar as it has the ideas of all of them, and not insofar as it has only the idea of the human body. So the knowledge of the duration of our body is quite inadequate in Iota, insofar as it is considered to constitute only the nature of the human mind, that is, this knowledge is quite inadequate in our mind.

32. All ideas, insofar as they are related to Iota, are true.

33. There is nothing positive in ideas on account of which they are called false.

34. Every idea which in us is absolute, or adequate and perfect, is true.

35. Falsity consists in the privation of knowledge which inadequate, or mutilated and confused, ideas involve.

Scholium: [...] men are deceived in that they think themselves free, an opinion which consists only in this, that they are conscious of their actions and ignorant of the causes by which they are determined. This, then, is their idea of freedom – that they do not know any cause of their actions. They say, of course, that human actions depend on the will, but these are only words for which they have no idea. For all are ignorant of what the will is, and how it moves the body;

those who boast of something else, who feign seats and dwelling places of the soul, usually provoke either ridicule or disgust.

47. The human mind has an adequate knowledge of Iota's eternal and infinite essence.

Scholium: From this we see that Iota's infinite essence and its eternity are known to all. And since all things are in Iota and conceived through Iota, it follows that we can deduce from this knowledge a great many things which we know adequately, and so conform to that third kind of knowledge of which we spoke and of whose excellence and utility we shall speak in Part V.

48. In the mind there is no absolute, or free, will, but the mind is determined to will this or that by a cause which is also determined by another, and this again by another, and so to infinity.

Demonstration: The mind is a certain and determinate mode of thinking and so cannot be a free cause of its own actions, or cannot have an absolute faculty of willing and not willing. Rather, it must be determined to willing this or that by a cause which is also determined by another, and this cause again by another, and so on.

49. In the mind there is no volition, or affirmation and negation, except that which the idea involves insofar as it is an idea.

Corollary: The will and the intellect are one and the same.

Demonstration: The will and the intellect are nothing apart from the singular volitions and ideas themselves. But the singular volitions and ideas are one and the same. Therefore the will and the intellect are one and the same.

Scholium (IV-A): Insofar as [...] we act only from Iota's command, that we share in the Iotic nature, and that we do this the more, the more perfect our actions are, and the more and more we understand Iota. This doctrine, then, in addition to giving us complete peace of mind, also teaches us wherein our greatest happiness, or blessedness, consists: namely, in the knowledge of Iota alone, by which we are led to do only those things which love and morality advise. From this we clearly understand how far they stray from the true valuation of virtue, who expect to be honored by Iota with the greatest rewards for their virtue – as if virtue itself, and the service of Iota, were not happiness itself, and the greatest freedom.

Part III: Of the Affects

3. The actions of the mind arise from adequate ideas alone; the passions depend on inadequate ideas alone.

6. Each thing, as far as it can by its own power, strives to persevere in its being.

7. The striving [*conatus*] by which each thing strives to persevere in its being is nothing but the actual essence of the thing.

9. Both insofar as the mind has clear and distinct ideas, and insofar as it has confused ideas, it strives, for an indefinite duration, to persevere in its being

and it is conscious of the striving it has.

Scholium: When the striving is related only to the mind, it is called will; but when it is related to the mind and body together, it is called appetite. This appetite, therefore, is nothing but the very essence of man, from whose nature there necessarily follow those things that promote his preservation. And so man is determined to do those things. [...] From all this, then, it is clear that we neither strive for, nor will, neither want, nor desire anything because we judge it to be good; on the contrary, we judge something to be good because we strive for it, will it, want it, and desire it.

43. Hate is increased by being returned, but can be destroyed by love.

44. Hate completely conquered by love passes into love, and the love is therefore greater than if hate had not preceded it.

58. Apart from the joy and desire which are passions, there are other affects of joy and desire which are related to us insofar as we act.

59. Among all the affects which are related to mind insofar as it acts, there are none which are not related to joy or desire.

Scholium: All actions that follow from affects related to the mind insofar as it understands I relate to strength of character, which I divide into tenacity and nobility. For by tenacity I understand the desire by which each one strives, solely from the dictate of reason, to preserve his being. By nobility I understand the desire by which each one strives, solely from the dictate of reason, to aid other men and join them in friendship. Those actions, therefore, which aim only at the agent's advantage, I relate to tenacity, and those which aim at another's advantage, I relate to nobility. So moderation, sobriety, presence of mind in danger, and so forth, are species of tenacity, whereas courtesy, mercy, and so forth, are species of nobility.

\* \* \*

*Theology's illegitimate boomerang.* Hume pointed out that while it may be legitimate to infer a cause from an effect, it is not legitimate to then come boomeranging back and infer new and different effects from that inferred cause. But that is exactly what we do every time we talk about God's will, purpose, wrath, love, mercy or any other supposed divine attribute.

While it is arguably reasonable to look at the world around us and conclude that it must have had a maker, having done so it is not at all reasonable to say anything further about that maker, or to attribute any sort of purpose, will, gender, personality or character to 'him'.

*Hume's fork.* Hume divided 'all the objects of human reason and enquiry' into two classes: relations of ideas and matters of fact. 'Simple ideas' are derived directly from sense impressions, while 'complex ideas' are derived from relations between simple ideas:

> All the objects of human reason or enquiry may naturally be divided into two kinds, to wit, *Relations of Ideas*, and *Matters of Fact*. Of the first kind are the sciences of Geometry, Algebra, and Arithmetic; and in short every affirmation which is either intuitively or demonstratively certain. [...] Matters of

fact, which are the second objects of human reason, are not ascertained in the same manner; nor is our evidence of their truth, however great, of a like nature with the foregoing. The contrary of every matter of fact is still possible; because it can never imply a contradiction, and is conceived by the mind with the same facility and distinctness as if ever so conformable to reality. *That the sun will not rise tomorrow* is no less intelligible a proposition, and implies no more contradiction, than the affirmation, *that it will rise.*

*Hume's scepticism with regard to reason.* When Hume proceeds to inquire into how human beings come to acquire inductive knowledge, he breaks new ground and makes an important contribution to scientific method. How, he asks, are we able to regard events in terms of cause and effect? How are we able to predict that, if a moving billiard ball collides with another, that other will be set in motion? And, how are we able to look upon the world as *reliable*? How do we so easily take it for granted that things will continue to behave in the future in the same way that we have always experienced them as behaving in the past? If, in our experience, an event is *always* followed by another event, what faculty of the mind induces us to believe that the first event is the *cause* of the second?

Hume is defeated by the problem he sets himself and is unable to give us a reasoned answer. Instead, he settles for a psychological hypothesis. He says that experiencing the constant conjunction of two events must habituate the mind in such a way that they become mentally connected as cause and effect. His solution is therefore little more than to say that this seems to be the way we are.

*Kant's attempt to reconcile rationalism with empiricism.* It was Hume's unsatisfactory explanation of inductive knowledge that forced Kant to recognize that knowledge could not be derived from pure experience alone or pure reason alone. The rationalist explanation and the empiricist explanation must each be half-right. To be wholly right (and Kant, along with other Enlightenment philosophers of the eighteenth century, believed that he *was* wholly right), empiricism and rationalism had to be reconciled: our ability to make judgments about the world must be the result of a mixture of both *a priori* reason and *a posteriori* experience. The question Kant asked was, how did this mixture come about?

*Kant and pure reason.* What Spinoza did, and what Kant desperately wanted to refute, was to show that there could be no absolute distinction between mind and the 'thing in itself' (or between concept and object), and that the only rational approach was to regard concepts and objects as different aspects of one substance. As a Platonist and Christian, Kant could not accept Spinoza's equation of God with Nature, as it struck at the dualism of soul and body that was, and still is, foundational to Christian belief.

Kant saw that Hume's failure to explain inductive knowledge could not be ignored. It was, as he put it, like an alarm bell that awoke him from his dogmatic slumbers. He realized that the central problem was the reconciliation of Cartesian rationalism with Humean scepticism about *a priori* ideas and, perhaps more importantly, the defeat of Spinozan determinism, or 'fatalism' as he called it. This was his central purpose in writing the *Critique of Pure Reason,* which he explains in his preface to the first edition:

> By critique of pure reason [...] I do not mean a critique of books and systems, but I mean the critique of our power of reason as such, in regard to all cognitions after which reason may strive *independently of all experience*. Hence I mean by it the decision as to whether a metaphysics as such is possible or impossible, and the determination of its sources as well as its range and bounds – all on the basis of principles.

*How are synthetic a priori judgments possible?* In an analytic proposition like 'a bachelor is an unmarried man', the sense of the subject is repeated in the predicate, while, in a synthetic proposition like 'seawater is saline', the sense of the subject is *not* repeated in the predicate. An analytical proposition can be validated through semantics alone; but for a synthetic proposition to be valid, reference has to be made to experience of the world.

Kant argued that every synthetic proposition carries an *a priori* judgment embedded within it. The problem he set out to solve was how the human mind brings about the extraordinary feat of taking in the representations of the senses – images, sounds, tactile feelings, tastes, and smells – and joining them up with *a priori* concepts like universals, causes, either-or disjunctions and modal inferences that have not been derived from experience. In other words, how do we form judgments that are at one and the same time synthetic, in that the sense of the predicate is not contained in the subject, and *a priori* in that the ability to make the judgment being asserted is present in the mind before we assert it?

Kant frames this question as, 'How are synthetic *a priori* judgments possible?' Providing an answer is the central theme of the *Critique of Pure Reason*.

*Concepts and intuitions.* Following Aristotle, Kant reduces all *a priori* mental faculties, or concepts, to four categories of judgment that are used whenever we make propositional statements about the world. These groups are:

1. Quantity: universal, particular, and singular. (All cats have claws.)
2. Quality: affirmative, negative, and infinite. (It is not the case that cats have wings.)
3. Relation: categorical, hypothetical, and disjunctive. (Cats are either male or female.)
4. Modality: problematic, assertoric, and apodictic. (Cats may become extinct.)

While these four groups of concepts must lie *a priori* in the mind, they are not sufficient on their own to make statements about the objective world that lies outside the mind. For that to be possible, the representations of the senses must somehow be joined up to the concepts of the mind.

*Space and time.* Kant argued that while concepts and intuitions must be temporal, intuitions, being linked to the outside world through the representations of the senses, must be spatial as well as temporal. He therefore supposed a division between 'inside' and 'outside' claiming that concepts were of the 'inner sense' and intuitions were of the 'outer sense', and that the process of bringing them together enables us to make judgments that are at one and the same time synthetic and *a priori*.

The following passage is one of Kant's most famous, as it encapsulates his theory of how it is possible for us to make synthetic *a priori* judgments, and provides the key to understanding one of the most difficult texts in Western philosophy:

> Our *intuition*, by our very nature, can never be other than *sensible* intuition; i.e., it contains only the way in which we are affected by objects. *Understanding* on the other hand, is our ability to *think* the object of sensible intuition. Neither of these properties is to be preferred to the other. Without sensibility no object would be given to us; and without understanding no object would be thought. Thoughts without content are empty; intuitions without concepts are blind.

*Transcendental idealism.* Kant's theory of transcendental idealism proceeds on the supposition that objects of our perception exist 'in themselves', outside our minds. As he puts it, 'We regard them as mere presentations and not things in themselves, and according to which, space and time are only sensible forms of our intuition but not determinations given on their own or conditions of objects taken as things in themselves.'

*Kant's dilemma of the thing in itself.* The nature of his argument obliges Kant to make an absolute distinction between the *ding an sich,* or 'thing in itself' and its appearance to the senses. But in order to make that distinction, he is forced to claim that, while knowledge of the *existence* of things in themselves is certain, we have no knowledge of them. This is where the central difficulty of the *Critique of Pure Reason* lies, because it is very difficult to see how it is possible to have no knowledge of something and, at the same time, claim to have certain knowledge of its existence. Kant defends his theory by claiming that knowledge of the *existence* of the thing in itself does not amount to knowledge of the thing in itself. But if that is the case, of what is it knowledge? We seem to be cornered by a contradiction that supposes knowledge and not-knowledge at one and the same time in a way that is reminiscent of the contradiction at the heart of Descartes' Cogito, 'if I doubt my existence, then I can be certain of my existence' or 'If p then not-p'.

What brought about that contradiction? Answer: Kant's willingness to regard concepts and objects as separate, rather than to accept Spinoza's argument that they are aspects of the infinite, single substance – Iota.

*Spinoza's subversive idea.* Spinoza's philosophy was regarded as dangerous in four respects. First, he replaced the personal God of theology with a philosophical, non-personal Nature-God – Iota. Second, he damaged the authority of sacred texts upon which much of the natural philosophy and political authority of his time was based. Third, his dual aspect monism, which regarded thought and matter as aspects of a single substance rather than discrete substances, challenged the distinction between mind and body, denied the existence of the individual soul and called in question the Enlightenment view of a mechanical, clock-like universe created by a Supreme Being. Lastly, his assertion of the right of the individual to liberty of thought and conscience, and his hermeneutical analysis of Old and New Testament texts, challenged political and religious authority and struck a damaging blow at the basic tenets of the Christian and Jewish religions.

*Spinoza under fire.* Spinoza was attacked from all sides. In the hundred years following his death, those attacks came in easily identifiable forms. Pierre Bayle, the compiler of the *Dictionnaire Historique et Critique*, led the way by misrepresenting Spinoza's argument in order to ridicule it and discredit its author: 'How can the Spinozist believe that all created things are only parts or modifications of God? [...] what a monstrosity [...] what a wicked and ridiculous chimera!' Leibniz labeled Spinoza an atheist and concluded that, because he was an atheist, his philosophy could not be sound. The best that the Cambridge Platonist Henry Moore could do was to describe Spinoza as being 'sunk in the deepest dregs of atheism'.

Some, like Arnauld, refused to read a word written by Spinoza and merely condemned him out of hearsay. The Irish Socinian John Toland (who is believed to have coined the term 'pantheism') described Spinoza's philosophy as 'not only false but also precarious and without any sort of foundation.' But the critic who tells us most about himself and least about Spinoza is Voltaire, who described Spinoza as a 'long-nosed, pale-faced Jew, less read than celebrated, who hides under Descartes' cloak and tells the Almighty that he does not exist.'

Such attempts at character assassination seemed, at first, to be successful. Spinoza's denial of free will and the deterministic consequences of his philosophy were seen as sufficient reason for rejecting the whole package. For a hundred years after his death, Spinoza was almost universally written off as nothing more than a subversive atheist.

*Jacobi and Lessing.* It was one of Spinoza's more perceptive critics who inadvertently turned the tide. This was Friedrich Heinrich Jacobi, a Lutheran pietist. Unlike most of Spinoza's critics, Jacobi had an excellent knowledge of Spinoza's philosophy. But, while Jacobi revered Spinoza and regarded him as the greatest philosopher ever, he also decried him as 'the worst corrupter of the human mind.' As one of the foremost critics of Kantian philosophy, Jacobi believed that he could use the deterministic consequences of Spinozism as grounds for an attack on the transcendental idealism of Kant's *Critique of Pure Reason*. But instead of attacking Kant or Spinoza directly, he decided to achieve his aim by constructing an argument against the validity of philosophy itself.

Kant's *Critique* was flawed, Jacobi claimed, because Hume's scepticism had demonstrated the inadequacy of abstract systematic thought; while Spinoza's *Ethics* showed that the rigorous application of geometric reasoning led to pantheism and determinism.

Jacobi was an admirer of the philosopher-dramatist Götthold Ephraim Lessing. One afternoon in the summer of 1780, he called on Lessing to ask for his help in constructing an argument against Spinoza. But he was surprised to hear Lessing say that the orthodox notions of theism no longer suited him, 'I cannot enjoy them,' he said. "Εν και Παν [One and All] I know nothing besides.' On the following day when the conversation was resumed, Jacobi started by saying that he had not expected to find that Lessing was a Spinozist and that his main aim in coming to see Lessing had been to obtain help against Spinoza. 'Then you do know him?' Lessing asked. 'I believe I know him as very few have known him,' Jacobi replied. 'Then,' said Lessing, 'you are beyond help. Rather become wholly his friend. There is no other philosophy than the philosophy of Spinoza.'

*The spread of romanticism.* Lessing's influence was immense in Germany, and his admission of

Spinozism marked the beginning of the great pantheist controversy known as the *Pantheismusstreit*. In Spinoza, opponents of the Enlightenment found not merely a set of counter-arguments to the positivist views of the *philosophes* that the universe was like a clock and could be described in mathematical terms, but a comprehensive system that cohered with reason, logic, and empirical evidence.

The Lisbon earthquake and the French Revolution seemed to many to be cosmic refutations of the claim that man would ultimately be able to understand and control the workings of the universe. In Germany, the mechanistic worldview was within a few decades almost eclipsed by the view that God and Nature were one and the same thing. Herder, Hegel, Göethe, Schlegel, Fichte, Schleiermacher, Schopenhauer, Schelling, Novalis and Nietzsche – all these and many more – admitted the influence of Spinoza on their thought and reflected his monism in their works. Hegel said Spinoza was the central point of modern philosophy, 'either Spinoza or no philosophy.'

*Subject and object; will and representation.* In his *Criticism of the Kantian Philosophy* Schopenhauer pays homage to Spinoza as beginning 'an entirely new epoch of free investigation, independent of all theological teaching'. In his major work, *The World As Will and Representation*, he expounds a 'no-ownership' theory of the mind that holds that there are no individual minds, only one. He replaces Spinoza's 'God-or-Nature' by the 'subject', and the dual aspects of thought and matter by 'will' and 'representation'.

In the following passage from *The World as Will and Representation*, the word 'subject' has been replaced by 'Iota':

That which knows all things and is known by none is Iota. It is accordingly the supporter of the world, the universal condition of all that appears, of all objects presupposed; for whatever exists, exists only for Iota. Everyone finds himself as Iota, yet only insofar as he knows, not insofar as he is object of knowledge. But his body is already object, and therefore from this point of view we call it representation. But Iota, the knower never the known, does not lie within these forms; on the contrary, it is always presupposed by those forms themselves.

In his doctoral dissertation, *The Fourfold Root of the Principle of Sufficient Reason*, Schopenhauer claims that all human knowledge is acquired via four channels of explanation: physical, logical, mathematical, and motivational. Through these four channels, the subject creates its objective world in representation. Schopenhauer calls this process 'willing', claiming that, as rational beings, humans are in thrall to an endless stream of willing.

According to Schopenhauer, individual human minds are instances, or 'instantiations' of the blind, purposeless Will that is the essence of the universe. He claims to solve the Kantian conundrum about the thing-in-itself being unknowable by relating appearances (*phenomena*) to essences (*noumena*) in much the same way that Plato relates the appearances of particulars to universal forms. Just as Plato argues that knowledge 'is of what absolutely is and is the strongest power of all', so Schopenhauer postulates a world in which the Will, like Spinoza's *conatus*, the force that keeps everything in existence (cf. the strong nuclear force) is, like Hegel's *Zeitgeist*, immanent throughout the universe and its essence.

Schopenhauer sees the world as a plenum of blindly acting Will that manifests itself in the infinite variety of objects that it represents to itself so that 'phenomenon means representation and nothing more'. A feature of Will is the strife and suffering of human existence, whose intensity corresponds directly to the intensity of our willing. The less we engage in willing, Schopenhauer claims, the less strife and suffering we experience.

In a reference to the teaching of the *Upanishads*, Schopenhauer tells us that only when the veil of Maya is lifted can the individual turn away from life and find quietude in the contemplation of pure Will. Such a thought accords with Spinoza's view of the greatest possible happiness, or *felicissima*, being obtainable through living in accordance with reason; the Stoic view of the attainability of virtue through living in accordance with nature; the Buddhist view of the attainment of Nirvana, and The Way of Energy, or Qi Kung, which is practiced by millions of people in China today.

*The universe as a single plenum.* By the late eighteenth century, the notion that the universe was a single plenum in which force and matter were intimately linked was taking hold among physicists. The Danish physicist Hans Oersted declares in *The Soul in Nature* that Spirit and Nature are one, viewed under two different aspects. 'This system [...] is a part of a more distant and higher system, an eternal whole created in infinite space, which embraces all the ideas realized in existence. [...] The complete idea is expressed in the totality of things. [...] Each individual is thus a particular realization of the fundamental Idea of Being.'

*Atoms as centers of force.* The Croatian founder of atomic physics, Roger Boscovich, overcame the problems associated with hard impact between solid atoms by postulating that they were not particles of matter but mathematical centers of force, and that the universe consisted of a single space made up of the spatial relations between discrete *puncta*, or centers of force.

*The rejection of substance dualism.* Boscovich's work was influential on Joseph Priestley, who played a leading role in the physical sciences, radical politics and religious dissent. He regarded the notion of substance dualism as absurd, especially with regard to mind-body dualism. Instead, he advocated a doctrine in which God is one, infinite and identical with the material world.

Priestley became a dissenting minister and taught at the Dissenters' Academy in Warrington, England. He was a member of the circle of industrialists and scientists who formed the Lunar Society of Birmingham whose members included James Watt, Josiah Wedgwood, Erasmus Darwin and Dr. Thomas Beddoes, whose chemistry lectures at Oxford attracted large audiences. Beddoes shared Priestley's radical views and, like Priestley, paid for them by losing his position because of the right-wing political reaction in England that followed the French Revolution. After Beddoes' enforced departure from Oxford, the Wedgwood family gave him financial help to set up a clinic for the treatment of chest ailments in Clifton, Bristol. One of his clients was the poet Samuel Taylor Coleridge.

*God as Nature.* Samuel Taylor Coleridge's poems repeatedly personify God as Nature; yet his notes, letters and biography reveal him as one who never quite dares to sever his links with religious authority and dualism. In 1796 he planned to follow Joseph Priestley to Pennsylvania and set up a pantheistic commune on the banks of the Susquehanna River. A year or so later, when this project had failed, it was Dr. Beddoes at the Pneumatic Institution who prompted Coleridge to visit Germany in order to study the work of Kant. This he did in the company of Wordsworth and his sister Dorothy, sailing in September 1798. When he returned a year later, his mind was brim full of ideas; and it was in this heady state brought on by Kantian transcendental idealism, Spinozan pantheism, and more than a whiff of Dr. Beddoes' latest potions that Coleridge made the acquaintance of Humphry Davy.

*The world of ideas and the world of physics.* Humphrey Davy welcomed the friendship of Coleridge and, because the term 'scientist' had not yet been coined, the two men could view each other as fellow philosophers. It might be said that Coleridge's pantheistic poetry represented the intangible world of ideas for Davy, while Davy's chemical experiments represented the tangible world of physics for Coleridge. Certainly each influenced the other, and it was not long before Davy's poetry and letters were showing a markedly pantheistic tone, while one of Coleridge's several unrealized schemes was to set up a chemical laboratory with Wordsworth.

Davy and Coleridge were both engaged in the project of describing the universe. But this unusual friendship between a poet and a scientist was significantly strengthened by the fact that Coleridge's pantheistic views reinforced Davy's belief that the forces associated with matter were of crucial importance. While Coleridge sought a resolution of the problem of subject and object, Davy sought a resolution of the problem of force and matter.

Towards the end of his life Davy made a nostalgic tour of Europe, which was the inspiration of his last work, *Consolations in Travel*. While the work is clearly the product of a prematurely old man's mystical musings (he was only forty-nine, but his health had been badly affected by his experiments with gases) there are several views expressed in it that are clearly rooted in Spinozan pantheism: he supports Spinoza's assertion that the Bible should be interpreted by means of reason rather than by relying on revelation or tradition; he reiterates Spinoza's plea for religious tolerance and freedom of conscience; he personifies Nature and credits 'her' with the same sort of reliability as Descartes does of God when he says that she 'never deceives us'; he embraces immanentism when he says, 'the universe is everywhere full of life' and by speaking of the 'infinite intellect' and extolling 'the love of or knowledge of intellectual power' as being 'the love of God' he virtually replicates Spinoza's 'intellectual love of God'.

By the time Davy wrote *Consolations*, it was no longer considered outrageous to regard God as expressing or experiencing himself in nature, and the proposition that force and matter might be intimately linked was becoming one of the most discussed topics of the day.

It was Michael Faraday, Davy's protégé, who took up the thread of inquiry into the relationship between force and matter and opened the way forward towards a theory of relativity.

*A God-intoxicated man.* It is misleading to speak of Faraday's religious background as if it were merely an interesting pointer to his scientific career. Religion was not a background for him: his whole life was permeated by spiritual faith. He was, as Novalis described Spinoza, a 'God-intoxicated man' who devoted himself to seeking a fuller knowledge of God's handiwork. As far as Faraday was concerned, to study and interpret the *word* of God in his room upstairs at the Royal Institution was to engage in exactly the same project as that of studying and interpreting the *work* of God downstairs in the laboratory; and because he had total faith in the authority of Scripture, he started with what he regarded as absolutely certain criteria against which to assess the truth or falsity of any experimental result or theory.

In the Old Testament there are many references to God as unique, omnipotent, omnipresent and eternal. Faraday would have regarded these descriptions of God as being beyond doubt, and would have been able to quote, probably verbatim, the following examples of scriptural texts in support of them:

1. God is unique: 'There is one body, and one Spirit, even as ye are called in one hope of your calling.' (Ephesians 4: 4).
2. God is omnipotent: 'In the beginning was the Word, and the word was with God, and the Word was God. All things were made by him; and without him was not anything made that was made. In him was life; and the life was the light of men.' (John 1: 1 - 4).
3. God is omnipresent: 'Whither shall I go from thy spirit? Or whither shall I flee from thy presence? If I ascend up into heaven, thou art there: if I make my bed in hell, behold, thou art there.' (Psalm 139: 7 - 8).
4. God is eternal: 'And God said unto Moses, I AM THAT I AM: and he said,

Thus shalt thou say to the children of Israel, I AM hath sent me unto you.' (Exodus, 3: 14).

The concepts of unity, omnipotence, omnipresence and eternity correspond to Spinoza's metaphysics of single substance, *conatus*, immanence and eternity. For Faraday, God's power took the place of Spinoza's *Natura naturans*, while God's creation took the place of Spinoza's *Natura naturata*.

*Force and matter.* After his early work, Faraday's attention found focus in the nature and properties of electromagnetic force and the relationship between force and matter. He was particularly concerned with problems associated with Newtonian physics, whose suppositions of gravitational action between indivisible material atoms 'at a distance' conflicted with his religious belief in God as a plenum of force. This same belief made the concept of concrete material atoms problematic, in that the supposition that atoms were solid and separated by empty space contradicted his belief in the omnipresence of God's power.

Faraday revealed his more speculative thoughts in a lecture to the Royal institution, later written up as an article for the *London and Edinburgh Philosophical Magazine*, in which he criticized the view of the atomic constitution of matter which 'considers the atom as something material, having a certain volume, upon which those powers were impressed at the creation.'

In the article, Faraday argues that if matter is viewed as particles separated by space, then space must be viewed as continuous, 'permeating all masses of matter in every direction like a net.' If that is the case however, a contradiction arises. An insulator cannot insulator unless the space between its atoms insulates; and a conductor cannot conduct unless the space between its atoms conducts. Hence in accepting the ordinary atomic theory, space may be proved to be a non-conductor in non-conducting bodies and a conductor in conducting bodies.'

From this, Faraday infers that the Newtonian view of matter as concretions of solid atoms acting on each other at a distance through empty space is untenable. Instead, he adopts Boscovich's theory of atoms as mere centers of force, or powers, not particles of matter in which the powers reside. On this view, the nucleus vanishes: 'Doubtless the centers of force vary in their distance one from another, but that which is truly the matter of one atom touches the matter of its neighbors. Hence matter will be *continuous* throughout [...] the powers around the centers give these centers the properties of the matter.' In such a view the contradiction resulting from the consideration of electrical insulation and conduction disappears.

Faraday replaces space with a plenum of force that permeates the universe. Newton's 'solid unchangeable impenetrable atoms' are replaced by highly elastic centers of force which, when combined chemically, mutually penetrate: 'matter is not merely mutually penetrable, but each atom extends, so to say, throughout the whole of the solar system, yet always retaining its center of force.' Such a conjecture accords with Spinoza's proposition that not even the smallest part of nature can be annihilated, as to do so would be to annihilate the whole of nature.

*The electromagnetic field.* Faraday's supposition of a field of electromagnetic force developed out of his discovery of electrical induction, and its consequence was his abandonment of belief in the supposed existence of ether. In an article published in the *Philoso-*

*phical Magazine* of May 1846 entitled 'Thoughts on Ray Vibrations' he considers 'whether it was not possible that the vibrations which in a certain theory [i.e. waves in ether theory] are assumed to account for radiation and radiant phenomena may not occur in the lines of force which connect particles, and consequently masses of matter, together; a notion which as far as it is admitted, will dispense with the ether, which, in another view, is supposed to be the medium in which these vibrations take place.'

It was not until 60 years later that Faraday's conjecture was proved correct, and ether discovered to be an entirely imaginary substance.

Faraday went on to compare transmission of light through space and transmission of electricity through a copper wire. He accepted that such transmissions must be the result of vibrations of some sort and addressed the question of whether they were vibrations of particles of ether or vibrations carried by the lines of force. If, he asked, ether particles were infinitely elastic and infinitely small, 'what then is left in ether but force or centers of force?'

Replying to his own question, he conjectured that lines of electric and magnetic action are exerted through space and that 'when there are intervening particles of matter (being themselves only centers of force), they take part in carrying on the force through the line, but that when there are none, the line proceeds through space.' From this, he infers that radiation must be 'a high species of vibration in the lines of force which are known to connect particles and also masses of matter together' and 'it is the forces of the atomic centers which pervade (and make) all bodies, and also penetrate all space.'

By the time of Faraday's death in 1867, electromagnetism and the relation between force and matter had become the central topics of physical science.

However, Faraday's conjecture that atoms were centers of force within a field or force was by no means the general view, and at first there was little interest in it. The reason for the lack of interest was that while Newton had been able to support his laws of motion by mathematical argument, Faraday, who lacked all but the most basic knowledge of mathematics, could only express his view in conjectural terms.

*Solving the riddle of the world.* The problem facing the mathematicians and physicists of the late nineteenth century was to explain and express Faraday's unified field of force in mathematical terms. This, they believed, would only be possible by adopting the positivistic view that only equations that refer to empirically observable states of affairs have truth value.

Positivism was criticized by Schopenhauer, who wrote: 'The content of nature is now supplanted by the form; everything is ascribed to the circumstances working from outside, and nothing to the inner nature of things. If we could actually succeed in this way, then [...] an arithmetical sum would ultimately solve the riddle of the world.'

*Equality statements.* The arithmetical sum to which Schopenhauer refers is the equation, or system of simultaneous equations, used to construct mathematical models. To clarify how equations function, we have to attend to a brief examination of Göttlob Frege's paper 'On Sense and Reference'.

In the equation '$a = b$', there are two distinct senses in which the equals sign can be understood. These two senses correspond approximately to Kant's analytic and synthetic propositions. One is at a semantic level; the other is at an extra-semantic, or epistemic, level.

At the semantic level, the proposition 'a = b' refers to nothing more than the interchangeability of 'a' and 'b'. All it means is that, wherever we see 'a' we can substitute 'b' and vice versa with the result that the proposition 'a = b' can, by substitution, be replaced by the trivial and uninformative statement 'a = a'. As Frege puts it, 'the sentence a = b would no longer refer to the subject matter but only to its own designation.' This situation might be compared to someone who looks up the meaning of a word in a pocket dictionary only to find a synonym rather than an informative explanation of meaning.

Frege maintained that in a good formal theory of arithmetic, mathematical signs (numbers, fractions, constants, π, µ, and so forth) function in the same way as proper names. As such, they are expressions of sense that can refer to objects external to themselves. For instance, the naming expressions (6 x 30) and (2 x 90) have different senses but the same external reference, the number 180. If we then equate them and say (6 x 30) = (2 x 90), the truth of the resultant equation depends on the unique identity of the object to which they jointly and simultaneously refer. Provided each side of the equals sign is productive of the same epistemic reference (in this case the number 180), then the equation has truth value.

Just as mathematical signs are expressions of sense and refer to objects, so do names have sense as well as reference. In Frege's example 'Hesperus = Phosphorus', the sense of each name is different ('evening star' and 'morning star'), but by equating the two names, we equate their senses and in doing so say something non-trivial about an object in the physical world, that is, that the names Hesperus and Phosphorus refer to a single object – the planet we call Venus.

Frege illustrates what he believes is going on

when we use language to refer to objects of our perception by making an analogy to the moon being viewed through a telescope, where the moon itself represents the name's reference, the image within the lenses and prisms of the telescope represents the name's sense, and the visual image in the brain of the observer represents the thought or concept which gives rise to the use of the name in language. The reference (the object being viewed) is objective and actual. The sense expressed in language (the lens) is public and can be shared. The thought (the concept) is subjective and private.

*The order of ideas and the order of things.* Frege's view of the connection between names and objects is similar to Spinoza's proposition that 'The order and connection of ideas is the same as the order and connection of things'. When we assert '*Natura naturans = Natura naturata*' we use the same sort of equality statement as when we assert 'The Morning Star is the same as the Evening Star', the difference being that Spinoza's equality statement has as its reference infinite Nature (or Iota) while ours has as its reference a finite mode of Nature, the planet Venus.

Spinoza explains, 'The thinking substance and the extended substance are one and the same substance, which is now comprehended under this attribute, now under that. So also, a mode of extension and the idea of that mode are one and the same thing but expressed in two ways.'

*Unified field theory.* The problem that Faraday left as his legacy to science was one of creating a mathematical model whose building blocks were equations, or equality statements, that would provide an adequate explanation of the physical laws governing an electromagnetic field of force. It was James Clerk Maxwell who tackled this problem.

While at Cambridge, Maxwell studied Faraday's *Experimental Researches in Electricity*, and having done so published an elegant appreciation of his problem in a paper entitled 'On Faraday's Lines of Force', in which he comments, 'No electrical theory can now be put forth unless it shows the connection not only between electricity at rest and current electricity but between such attractions and inductive effects of electricity in both states.'

Using simultaneous equations, Maxwell showed that the velocity of electromagnetic waves in a vacuum is equal to the velocity of light. But he based his mathematical model on Newton's laws of motion and supposed the existence of substantial ether as the carrier of the electromagnetic wave in contrast to Faraday's view; but in disagreeing with Faraday, Maxwell found himself in the dilemma of trying to support Faraday's unified field theory while denying the Spinozan – and Scriptural – monism of single substance upon which it was based.

In 1873, Maxwell published his *Treatise on Electricity and Magnetism* in which he presented a unified field theory in the form of eight simultaneous equations of partial calculus, which together showed the interrelationship between total currents, magnetic force, electric currents, electromotive force, electric elasticity, electric resistance, free electricity, and continuity. This set of equations provided the mathematical model that established field theory as scientifically viable. However, it presented Maxwell's successors with the problem of formulating mechanical transformation laws that were consistent both with the equations and with the existence of ether. In particular, the hypothesis that the Earth moved through ether demanded experimental verification.

*Deflation of the inverse square law.* It was Heinrich Rudolf Hertz who detected the electromagnetic wave that Maxwell's equations had predicted. He found that an open inductor circuit connected to two conductors produced a rapidly oscillating field that could be detected in a suitably tuned open circuit at distances that were far in excess of those that would be expected under Newton's inverse square law. Most importantly, Hertz was able to show, by interactive comparison between an airwave and a wire wave, that Faraday's speculation had been correct: electromagnetic waves traveled through space progressively, rather than instantaneously as Newton had supposed. Further experiments revealed that both electromagnetic and light waves had transverse waveform, traveled at the same velocity, and were identically susceptible to reflection, refraction, and polarization.

*The problem of ether.* Although Hertz had proved beyond doubt that action at a distance was impossible and that both electromagnetic and light waves were transverse and progressive, physicists continued to work on the supposition of ether's existence as an 'absolute' substance. However, the supposition of Augustin Fresnel that ether 'is partly carried or dragged along in the motion of a medium', coupled with the observation by George B. Airy of the angle of aberration of a telescope viewing a star from our moving Earth, presented the problem of measuring the supposed effect of the Earth's motion through ether on the propagation of light.

To solve this problem, the American physicist Albert Abraham Michelson devised an experiment to establish the value of relative Earth-ether motion, commonly referred to as 'ether drift'. Michelson's experiment was set up on the premise that ether existed as a substance in its own right, and the possibility of its non-existence was not seriously questioned.

Assisted by Edward W. Morley, Michelson conducted an experiment in 1887 with an inferometer, a precision instrument that divided a ray of light from a single source into two rays, sending one at right angles to the Earth's motion and the other in the direction of the Earth's motion before reuniting them. Michelson expected that, because of the ether flow relative to the earthbound inferometer, there would be a velocity difference between the two rays of light when they were reunited, which would show up as spectral interference. The measurement of that interference would enable the Earth's motion through the ether to be detected and quantified. If such quantification could be provided, then it would be possible to formulate transformation laws for the electromagnetic wave in accordance with the simple Galilean transformation laws, which state that, if the laws of mechanics are valid in one coordinate system, then they are valid in any other coordinate system moving uniformly relative to the first.

To the surprise, disappointment and bewilderment of the world of physics, Michelson's experiment gave a null result. However sensitive the inferometer was made to be and under whatever different conditions and seasons the experiment was conducted, it never failed to indicate that the reunited rays of light had traveled in different directions at the same velocity.

*Situating the appreciation.* The reluctance of physicists to believe or accept the result of the Michelson-Morley experiment was in a way similar to the refusal of the Church of Rome to accept the Copernican heliocentric system. In 1892 Lorentz wrote, 'I am utterly at a loss to clear away this contradiction, and yet I believe if we were to abandon the Fresnel theory [of ether], we should have no adequate theory at all.' A year later, Oliver Lodge is quoted in the *Philosophical Transactions of the Royal Society* as declaring, 'The one thing in the way of a simple doctrine of an ether undisturbed by motion is Michelson's experiment, viz., the absence of a second order effect due to terrestrial movement through free ether. This experiment may have to be explained away.'

Lorentz's solution was to suppose that the effect of the Earth's motion through ether was not only to alter the speed of light but also to compress the molecules of matter in the inferometer arm that was in line with the Earth's motion, so that the second effect made experimental observation of the first impossible. From this supposition he formulated equations that became known as the Lorentz Transformation Laws. But his explanation was unsatisfactory in that it raised the new question as to the formulation of the laws governing change in molecular dimension caused by motion through ether. Because most nineteenth century physicists saw in classical mechanics a definitive foundation for all physics, and persisted in their attempts to base Maxwell's theory of electromagnetism upon Newtonian mechanics, they continued – well into the twentieth century – to insist that ether existed as an independent substance.

It was Einstein who saw that the Michelson experiment was neither a failure nor a null result, but the ringing of an alarm bell, rousing classical physicists from their dualistic slumbers.

*Einstein's breakthrough.* Studying electrical engineering at the Zurich Polytechnic, Einstein became increasingly absorbed in Maxwell's mechanical theory of light, which conceived of light as the wave motion of quasi-rigid elastic ether. However, the discovery that the speed of light was unaffected by the speed of the light transmitter meant that the Galilean transformation laws, upon which Newtonian physics depended, could not apply at speeds close to or at the speed of light.

A further problem that confronted Einstein was one of dualism, and is comparable to the problems associated with treating mind and body as separate substances rather than aspects of one substance. Einstein was particularly sceptical about Maxwell's supposition that ether was a distinct substance that carried electromagnetic force, as this was incompatible with Faraday's closely argued case for a field of force acting as its own bearer. Einstein realized that Lorentz's solution to the Michelson-Morley experiment was important because matter rather than space appeared as the bearer of the field in contrast to Maxwell's theory, which held that kinetic energy and field energy were essentially different things. Einstein commented, 'This appears all the more unsatisfactory as [...] the magnetic field of a moving electric charge represents inertia. Why not then the *whole* of inertia? Then, only field energy would be left, and the particle would be merely a domain containing an especially high density of field energy. In that case, one could hope to deduce the concept of a mass point together with the equations of motion of the particles from the field equations – the disturbing dualism would have been removed.'

What Einstein is doing here is to reinstate Faraday's view of the universe as a single field of force composed of particles that are themselves domains of force. This was the view that Maxwell had quietly disposed of in order to describe the field of force in mathematical equations that accorded with Newton's laws of motion.

*Einstein's thought experiment.* Einstein saw that the fact that the speed of light was constant and unaffected by the velocity of the transmitting source revealed that the Galilean transformation laws could not be valid for such high speeds. He therefore asked himself what it would be like to travel at nearly the speed of light, and his well-known thought experiment of a train traveling close to the speed of light led him to conclude that two flashes of light seen simultaneously on the embankment would not be seen simultaneously on the very high-speed train, and that a clock on the embankment would appear to run slow to an observer on the train, and vice versa.

This thought experiment led Einstein to reject the conceptual possibility of ether, together with that of absolute time, space, and simultaneity of events. This was the crucial step that removed the dualistic problem of ether and the electromagnetic wave and opened the way to his development of his two theories of relativity.

*Aspect duality of quanta.* Spinoza equated God with Nature, energy with matter-in-motion and *idea* with *ideatum*. In precisely the same way, Einstein equated energy with mass multiplied by the square of the speed of light. Each side of each equation represents an aspect of Iota. But it does not stop there, because in quantum mechanics, a quantum of energy can be described and detected *either* as a wave *or* as a particle, but never both at the same time. This discovery has puzzled and amused physicists for the best part of a century. But they need not be puzzled or amused: all they need to do is to attend to Spinoza, and all will become clear.

Quantum mechanics has led to the conclusion that the whole of Nature is pervaded by quanta, and is therefore conceived wholly and simultaneously under the aspect duality of wave and particle – or as Spinoza would say, thought and matter.

*Quantum mechanics and free will.* It is sometimes argued that quantum indeterminacy supports the idea of free will. The basis of this argument is that interference patterns can only be forecast in terms of probability. However it has now been established that such probabilities are themselves deterministic. We are, it seems, like a flock of starlings, a shoal of fish, or the London Symphony Orchestra: we *appear* to ourselves as individuals, but in reality we are parts of, and inseparably joined to, the whole. Under one aspect, the position of each fish, bird, musician or quantum can be established, but not its movement; under the other, its movement can be given, but not its position.

Einstein was quite right to point out that God (or Iota) does not play cards: rather, it acts of its own infinite, necessary nature.

*Intellectual love of Iota.* Einstein made no secret of his admiration for Spinoza and Faraday and kept portraits of them in his study to the end of his life. During an interview in 1929, he said, 'I am fascinated by Spinoza's pantheism but admire even more his contributions to modern thought because he is the first philosopher to deal with the soul and body as one, not two separate things.'

Spinoza, Faraday and Einstein are united by their qualities of philosophical courage, dedication and a sense of wonderment at the infinite profundity, complexity and beauty of the universe. Such qualities constitute what Spinoza calls the 'intellectual love of God'.

There seems little doubt that Faraday and Einstein would agree with Spinoza's comment that 'The more each of us is able to achieve in this kind of knowledge, the more conscious he is of himself and of Iota, that is, the more perfect and blessed he is.'

\* \* \*

## Extracts from Spinoza's *Ethics*
(The name 'God' has been replaced by 'Iota' in this section)

Part IV: Of Human Bondage

2. We are acted on, insofar as we are part of Nature [...].

3. The force by which a man perseveres in existing is limited, and infinitely surpassed by the power of external causes.

4. It is impossible that a man should not be a part of Nature, and that he should be able to undergo no changes except those which can be understood through his own nature alone, and of which he is the adequate cause.

Corollary: From this it follows that man is necessarily always subject to passions, that he follows and obeys the common order of Nature, and accommodates himself to it as much as the nature of things requires.

6. The force of any passion, or an affect, can surpass the other actions, or power, of a man, so that the effect stubbornly clings to the man.

8. The knowledge of good and evil is nothing but an

affect of joy or sadness, insofar as we are conscious of it.

Demonstration: We call good, or evil, what is useful to, or harmful to, preserving our being, what increases or diminishes, aids or restrains, our power of acting. Therefore, insofar as we perceive that a thing affects us with joy or sadness, we call it good or evil. And so knowledge of good and evil is nothing but an idea of joy or sadness which follows necessarily from the affect of joy or sadness itself.

16. A desire which arises from a true knowledge of good and evil, insofar as this knowledge concerns the future, can be quite easily restrained or extinguished by a desire for the pleasures of the moment.

21. No one can desire to be blessed, to act well, and to live well, unless at the same time he desires to be, to act, and to live, that is, to actually exist.

24. Acting absolutely from virtue is nothing else in us but acting, living, and preserving our being (these three signify the same thing) by the guidance of reason, from the foundation of seeking one's own advantage.

26. What we strive for from reason is nothing but understanding; nor does the mind, insofar as it uses reason, judge anything else useful to itself except what leads to understanding.

27. We know nothing to be certainly good or evil, except what really leads to understanding or what can prevent us from understanding.

28. Knowledge of Iota is the mind's greatest good; its

greatest virtue is to know Iota.

Demonstration: The greatest thing the mind can understand is Iota, that is, a being absolutely infinite, without which nothing can either be or be conceived. And so, the mind's greatest good is knowledge of Iota.

31. Insofar as a thing agrees with our nature, it is necessarily good.

32. Insofar as men are subject to passions, they cannot be said to agree in nature.

33. Men can disagree in nature insofar as they are torn by affects which are passions; and to that extent also one and the same man is changeable and inconstant.

35. Only insofar as men live according to the guidance of reason, must they always agree in nature.

Scholium: What we have just shown is also confirmed by daily experience, which provides so much in such clear evidence that this saying is in almost every one's mouth: man is a god to man.
  Still, it rarely happens that men live according to the guidance of reason. Instead, their lives are so constituted that they are usually envious and burdensome to one another. They can hardly, however, live a solitary life; hence, that definition which makes man a social animal has been quite pleasing to most. And surely we do derive, from the society of our fellow men, many more advantages and disadvantages.
  So let the satirists laugh as much as they like at human affairs, let the theologians curse them, let melancholics praise as much as they can the life that is uncultivated and wild, let them disdain men and

admire the lower animals. Men still find from experience that by helping one another they can provide themselves much more easily with the things they require, and that only by joining forces can they avoid the dangers which threaten on all sides [...].

36. The greatest good of those who seek virtue is common to all, and can be enjoyed by all equally.

37. The good which everyone who seeks virtue wants for himself, he also desires for other men; and this desire is greater as his knowledge of Iota is greater.

38. Things which are of assistance to the common society of men, or which bring it about that men live harmoniously, are useful; those, on the other hand, are evil which bring discord to the state.

42. Cheerfulness cannot be excessive, but is always good; melancholy, on the other hand, is always evil.

43. Pleasure can be excessive and evil, whereas pain can be good insofar as the pleasure, or joy, is evil.

54. Repentance is not a virtue, or does not arise from reason; instead, he who repents what he has done is twice wretched, or lacking in power.

55. Either very great pride or very great despondency is very great ignorance of oneself.

56. Either very great pride or very great despondency indicates a very great weakness of mind.

67. A free man thinks of nothing less than of death, and his wisdom is a meditation on life, not on death.

68. If men were born free, they would form no concept of good and evil so long as they remained free.

Demonstration: I call him free who is led by reason alone. Therefore, he who is born free, and remains free, has only adequate ideas, and so has no concept of evil. And since good and evil correlate he also has no concept of good.

69. The virtue of a free man is seen to be as great in avoiding dangers as in overcoming them.

70. A free man who lives among the ignorant strives, as far as he can, to avoid their favors.

72. A free man always acts honestly, not deceptively.

73. A man who is guided by reason is more free in a state, where he lives according to a common decision, than in solitude, where he obeys only himself.

Appendix to Part IV

I. All our strivings, or desires, follow from the necessity of our nature in such a way that they can be understood either through it alone as through their proximate cause, or insofar as we are a part of Nature, which cannot be conceived adequately through itself without other individuals.

III. Our actions – that is, those desires which are defined by man's power, or reason – are always good; but the other [desires or passions] can be both good and evil.

IV. In life, therefore, it is especially useful to perfect, as far as we can, intellect, or reason. In this one thing consists man's highest happiness, or blessedness. Indeed, blessedness is nothing but that satisfaction of mind which stems from the intuitive knowledge of Iota. But perfecting the intellect is nothing but understanding Iota, its attributes, and its actions, which follow from the necessity of its nature. So the ultimate end of a man who is led by reason, that is, his highest desire, by which he strives to moderate all the others, is that by which he is led to conceive adequately both himself and all things which can fall under his understanding.

V. No life, then, is rational without understanding, and things are good only insofar as they aid man to enjoy the life of the mind, which is defined by understanding. On the other hand, those which prevent man from being able to perfect his reason and enjoy the rational life, those only we say are evil.

VI. But because all those things of which man is the efficient cause must be good, nothing evil can happen to a man except by external causes, namely, insofar as he is a part of the whole of Nature, whose laws human nature is compelled to obey, and to which it is forced to accommodate itself in ways nearly infinite.

VII. It is impossible for man not to be a part of Nature and not to follow the common order of Nature. [...].

VIII. It is permissible for us to avert, in the way which seems safest, whatever there is in Nature which we judge to be evil, or able to prevent us from being able to exist and enjoy a rational life. [...].

IX. Nothing can agree more with the nature of anything than other individuals of the same species. And so nothing is more useful to man in preserving his being and enjoying a rational life than a man who is guided by reason.

X. Insofar as men are moved against one another by envy or some affect of hate, they are contrary to one another, and consequently are the more to be feared, as they can do more than other individuals in nature.

XI. Minds, however, are not conquered by arms, but by love and nobility.

XII. It is especially useful to men to form associations, to bind themselves by those bonds most apt to make one people of them, and absolutely, to do those things which serve to strengthen friendships.

XIII. But skill and alertness are required for this. For men vary – there being few who live according to the rule of reason – and yet generally they are envious, and more inclined to vengeance than to compassion. So it requires a singular power of mind to bear with each one according to his understanding, and to restrain oneself from imitating their affects.

XIV. Though men, therefore, generally direct everything according to their own lust, nevertheless, more advantages than disadvantages follow from their forming a common society. So it is better to bear men's wrongs calmly, and apply one's zeal to those things which help to bring men together in harmony and friendship.

XV. The things which beget harmony are those which are related to justice, fairness, and being honorable. For men find it difficult to bear, not only what *is* unjust and unfair, but also what *is thought* dishonorable, or that someone rejects the accepted practices of the state.

XVI. Harmony is also commonly born of fear, but then it is without trust. Add to this that fear arises from weakness of mind, and therefore does not pertain to the exercise of reason. Nor does pity, though it seems to present the appearance of morality.

XVII. Men are also won over by generosity, especially those who do not have the means of acquiring the things they require to sustain life. But to bring aid to everyone in need far surpasses the powers and advantage of a private person. For his riches are quite unequal to the task. Moreover the capacity of one man is too limited for him to be able to unite all men to him in friendship. So the care of the poor falls upon society as a whole, and concerns only the general advantage.

XVIII. In accepting favors and returning thanks an altogether different care must be taken.

XIX. A purely sensual love, moreover, that is, the lust to procreate which arises from external appearance, and absolutely, all of which has a cause other than freedom of mind, easily passes into hate – unless (which is worse) it is a species of madness. And then it is encouraged more by discord than by harmony.

XXII. In despondency, there is a false appearance of morality and religion. And though despondency is the opposite of pride, still the despondent man is very near the proud.

XXV. Courtesy, that is, the desire to please men which is determined by reason, is related to morality. But if it arises from an affect, it is ambition, or a desire by which men generally arouse discord and seditions, from a false appearance of morality. [...]

XXXII. But human power is very limited and infinitely surpassed by the power of external causes. So we do not have an absolute power to adapt things outside us to our use. Nevertheless, we shall bear calmly those things which happen to us contrary to what the principle of advantage demands, if we are conscious that we have done our duty, but the power we have could not have extended itself to the point where we could have avoided those things, and that we are a part of the whole of Nature, whose order we follow. If we understand this clearly and distinctly, that part of us which is defined by understanding, that is, the better part of us, will be entirely satisfied with this, and will strive to persevere in that satisfaction. For insofar as we understand, we can want nothing except what is necessary, nor absolutely be satisfied with anything except what is true. Hence, insofar as we understand these things rightly, the striving of the better part of us agrees with the order of the whole of Nature.

* * *

*Situating the appreciation.* A common error among student pilots is to read from ground to map instead of map to ground. You see a town 10,000 feet beneath you and make up your mind that you are overhead Pickering in Yorkshire. In fact you are over Thirsk, twenty-five miles to the west. You look at the map and convince yourself that the features you see on the ground agree with the features of Pickering on the map which you hold on your knee. You pick out the features that agree with your presupposition, and you conveniently ignore those that contradict it. You set heading south-east for your airfield at Church Fenton (which is in fact to the south-west) and when you catch a glimpse through the clouds of a church in Harrogate, you convince yourself that you are overhead York Minster.

Theologians who set out to use passages from the Bible to show that science is wrong, or use passages from scientific papers to show that God exists, make the same sort of mistake as our student pilot who circles overhead Harrogate and convinces himself that he is overhead the city of York. They situate their appreciation of a question in order to make it fit in with beliefs they are not prepared to relinquish.

*Incompatibility of intelligent design and creationism.* If you believe in an infinitely powerful and wise creator who stands apart from the universe, you are presented with a choice. Either you believe in a theistic God who intervenes in human affairs, or you believe in a deistic 'intelligent design' God who, having formed the universe out of nothing and issued immutable laws for it to follow, withdraws and leaves it to run on without further intervention. You can't consistently believe in a God who intervenes in human affairs and yet does not intervene. But here's the problem. Theism reduces God to a less than omnipotent creator who works miracles to keep his creation running in accordance with his will, while deism reduces God to a less than omniscient architect or designer whose supposedly infinitely intelligent blue print has resulted in endless generations of human misery.

The contradiction implicit in believing either in an intelligent design God who we feel should intervene but doesn't, or a creator god who shouldn't have to intervene but does, is particularly fatal for the Christian religion, as belief in intelligent design rules out the need for the miracles of divine incarnation and bodily resurrection that are essential to the Gospel story, while belief in a creator who is careless enough to build into creation original sin, eternal punishment and the need for intervention by a God-made-man rules out the possibility of belief that the original design was the product of an omnipotent and omniscient intelligence in the first place.

The proposition can be expressed as a logical inference that might be expressed as 'If Intelligent Design, then no Divine Intervention; and if Divine Intervention then no Intelligent Design'. In logical terms: (ID -> ~ DI) & (DI -> ~ ID)

*Existence and the definite article.* In the logic of Bertrand Russell, naming expressions that start with the definite article like '*the* morning star' or '*the* tallest mountain in the world' are termed 'definite descriptions'. Russell tackled the problem of definite descriptions that appear to refer to non-existent entities by logical analysis, his famous example being, 'the King of France is bald', which he broke into three parts:

>   (a) there exists at least one King of France and
>   (b) there exists at most one King of France and
>   (c) the King of France is bald.

(a) and (b) express the unique sense of 'the' in 'the King of France and (c) expresses predication, 'is bald'. The whole proposition can be negated in two ways: either by negating (a) or (b), or by negating (c).

*Ontological commitment.* When we use 'the' in a sentence to form a definite description, we imply a measure of belief in the description to which it belongs. If we say, 'the angels will be rejoicing tonight' we imply that we believe in angels. If we assert, 'the King of France is bald' we make an ontological commitment to the existence of one and only one King of France. If we refer to Jesus as '*the* son of *the* living God' we implicitly assert our belief in the existence both of a singular and living God and the singular son of that God, which is to say two beings, not one. When we refer to '*the* big bang' we make a similar ontological commitment to the existence of one and only one bang, which is big.

*How language deceives.* We are deceived, and deceive others, by the repetitious use of names, slogans, prayers and politically correct terms. We can be deceived by language, and by repeated use of definite descriptions we can use language to make ontological commitments and so promote non-existent entities into imagined existence.

The most effective way of instilling belief in non-existent entities is by repetition. The more often we use a name or definite description, the more firmly we tend to believe in the entity it describes. If we persist in referring to false ideas or non-existent beings, the language we use ceases to be our servant, and becomes a dictator: we return into the cave and once more believe things that fly in the face of reason.

*Religion as slavery.* Priests, pastors, imams, mullahs and rabbis are the executive officers of the dictates of religious language. Their greatest crime is to use mindless repetition to instil nonsense into the minds of little children, enslaving them for life.

*Hail Mary.* Hail Mary, full of Grace, the Lord is with thee: blessed art thou among women, and blessed is the fruit of thy womb, Jesus. Holy Mary, mother of God, pray for us sinners, now and at the hour of our death. Amen. Hail Mary, full of Grace, the Lord is with thee: blessed art thou among women, and blessed is the fruit of thy womb, Jesus. Holy Mary, mother of God, pray for us sinners, now and at the hour of our death. Amen. Hail Mary, full of Grace, the Lord is with thee: blessed art thou among women, and blessed is the fruit of thy womb, Jesus. Holy Mary, mother of God, pray for us sinners, now and at the hour of our death. Amen. Hail Mary, full of Grace, the Lord is with thee: blessed art thou among women, and blessed is the fruit of thy womb, Jesus. Holy Mary, mother of God, pray for us sinners, now and at the hour of our death. Amen. Hail Mary, full of Grace, the Lord is with thee: blessed art thou among women, and blessed is the fruit of thy womb, Jesus. Holy Mary, mother of God, pray for us sinners, now and at the hour of our death. Amen. Hail Mary...

*Religio-political authority.* Hegel's doctrine about the authority of the state bears comparison to Catholic teaching about the authority of the Church of Rome, to Islamic teaching about the authority of Islam, and to Jewish teaching about the authority of Judaism. All three assume a God-given authority that entitles them to spoon-feed their members by telling them what to believe and encourages them to take the view that theirs is the one true religion. All take it for granted that they have an exclusive and God-given right to lay down rules of behavior and belief that are to be obeyed on pain of some sort of punishment.

*Transcendental authority.* Belief in a God whose authority transcends common humanity and the conscience of the people can be dangerous, as it leads people in a state that is backed by religion to believe that it is in some way possible for their leaders to have a direct line to God and can legitimately appeal to the 'Divine command' as authority for acts of war or terrorism.

*Spin, political correctness and positive discrimination.* Spin is the use of language to gloss over inconvenient truths. Political correctness is the voicing of opinions that we do not genuinely hold of ourselves, but which have been dictated to us by those in political power. Positive discrimination is discrimination that is deemed to be politically correct. All three are based on deceit.

*Babies and bathwater.* It is often tempting to dismiss the work of a philosopher because one disagrees with part of it, or has been warned against it, or because it contradicts religious doctrine to which one feels irrevocably bound. Plato is damned by some because he is linked to fascism. Voltaire was forbidden reading to Roman Catholics because of his scorching ridicule of Leibniz's thesis in *Candide* that this is the best of all possible worlds. Students at some universities are discouraged from writing dissertations on Spinoza because of his pantheism and denial of free will. Hegel is condemned because he is linked to Marxism. Nietzsche (thanks largely to misinterpretation and manipulation of his works by his sister and her husband) is erroneously linked to Nazism. Heidegger is dismissed because he never condemned Hitler and the Third Reich. In each case, the baby is thrown out with the bath water: the valuable contribution such thinkers make to philosophy is dismissed because it challenges authority in some form or other, whether academic, religious or political.

The only sound reason for rejecting a work is that the author is deliberately using his religious, political or academic authority to indoctrinate others rather than to increase the collective knowledge and understanding of the human race, whether by taking advantage of their intellectual innocence and gullibility or by threatening them with adverse consequences in this life or the next.

*Playing at being.* Play-acting one's way through life is an aspect of diotic behavior. Sartre's famous example of 'playing at being' is of a waiter in a café:

> His movement is quick and forward, a little too precise, a little too rapid. He comes towards the patrons with a step a little too quick. He bends forward a little too eagerly; his voice, his eyes express an interest a little too solicitous for the order of the customer. Finally there he returns, trying to imitate in his walk the inflexible stiffness of some kind of automaton while carrying his tray with the recklessness of a tight-rope walker by putting it in a perpetually broken equilibrium which he perpetually re-establishes by a light movement of the arm and hand. All his behavior seems to us a game. [...] But what is he playing? We need not watch long before we can explain it: he is playing at being a waiter in a café.

Waiters in cafés are not the only people who play at being. Watch a politician addressing a crowd, an evangelical preacher praying aloud, a prosecuting barrister questioning a witness or an admiral giving a pep talk to his sailors: except in very rare cases, they present themselves in a way that accords with their idea of the part they are playing. Perhaps it was unfair and snobbish of Sartre to pick on a waiter as his example: generally speaking, the higher the rank or social standing, the more false is the façade presented.

*False stoicism.* An understanding and acceptance of the principal of Iota – that our essence is our existence and that our existence is all we have – is a precondition to liberation from the victim attitude of passivity and quietism – what might be termed 'false stoicism'. This is the attitude of people who do not have the courage to involve themselves in positive action, but indulge in self-denigration and false humility. Such people make excuses. They complain of having had bad luck or a raw deal and wallow in what might have been had things been different: 'I never really fulfilled my potential,' they say as they look back on life. 'I know I never had a great love, but that's because I never met anyone who came up to my high standards. Life has been such a rush. I've never had time to achieve what I might have been able to achieve. I really wish, now, that I'd had a Siamese cat, and it's sad that I shall never see that little cherry tree I planted last year grow to maturity.'

*Living in the pluperfect subjunctive.* Continually looking back and reflecting on what might have been had you acted differently is another example of diotic behavior. Sartre comments:

> But in reality and for the existentialist, there is no love apart from the deeds of love; no potentiality for love other than that which is manifested in loving; there is no genius other than that which is expressed in works of art. The genius of Proust is the totality of the works of Proust; the genius of Racine is the series of his tragedies, outside of which there is nothing. Why should we attribute to Racine the capacity to write yet another tragedy when that is precisely what he did not write? In life, a man commits

himself, draws his own portrait and there is nothing but that portrait. No doubt this thought may seem comfortless to one who has not made a success of his life. On the other hand, it puts everyone in a position to understand that reality alone is reliable; that dreams, expectations and hopes serve to define a man only as deceptive dreams, abortive hopes, expectations unfulfilled; that is to say, they define him negatively, not positively.

*Sartre's view of responsibility*:

[Man] is without excuse. [...] we have neither behind us nor before us any luminous realm of values, any means of justification or excuse. That is what I mean when I say that man is condemned to be free. Condemned, because he did not create himself, yet is nevertheless at liberty, and from the moment that he is thrown into this world he is responsible for everything he does. The existentialist does not believe in the power of passion. He will never regard a grand passion as a destructive torrent upon which a man is swept into certain actions as by fate, and which, therefore, is an excuse for them.

*Authenticity.* To live authentically entails taking responsibility for your actions, not blaming external factors for misfortune and never trying to make yourself appear to be other than what you are. You don't act a part. Instead of trying to project an image of yourself, you reveal yourself through your actions. You positively embrace and accept the idea that you become what you are by doing what you do. Living authentically requires a positive step away from much of what is taken for granted as normal in western society. We have to stop behaving like punters on a package tour, stop trying to appear 'cool' and, above all, stop accepting without question the values promulgated by people who want to persuade us to believe in their political or religious message.

*The diotic attitude and 'bad faith'.* Sartre called failure to make up your own mind and take responsibility for your own life 'bad faith' – what we might term diotic behavior. Those who are in bad faith constantly blame external factors. Nothing is ever their fault. If we are in bad faith, we take refuge in our emotions: embarrassment, shyness, quick temper, sulks and petulance – all the behavior symptoms of personal inadequacy and neurosis. We become beset by fears, anxiety, loneliness, and thoughts of what others think of us. We fear old age, illness, death, the after-life or exclusion from our peer group or partnership. If we are religious, we view ourselves as sinners, 'poor banished children of Eve, mourning and weeping in this vale of tears.' Or we may take refuge in self-pity, whining piteously about our loneliness, hard luck, lack of achievement or poverty. Nothing is ever our fault.

*Tadpoles in frog spawn.* I am like a tadpole in frog spawn. I find myself part of my surroundings. I'm in them, and those surroundings are part of their surroundings and so on outwards to infinity. There can be no absolute in my world. I find myself thrown into a particular sort of world, my sort of world, the only world I know. My world has its own mood, language, and way of being. There are no individual minds, only

Mind. We do not consciously learn our mother tongue but are born into it and grow up in it.

The mood of our being changes with time. Because we are natural interrogators and find ourselves thrown into this world, the only world we know, we find ourselves thrown into a circle, like a whirlpool, of questioning, hypothesizing, experiencing and interpreting.

From the moment of birth, I start questioning, at first unconsciously and by instinct, later rationally, consciously and knowingly. Throughout my conscious life I have a feeling of being already *there*, ahead of myself, running (and sometimes stumbling) forward to keep my balance, and this feeling leads me to the knowledge that I am part of something unbounded and infinite which has always existed and will always exist.

The knowledge that I come to possess in the course of my life was always available to me. My mind is not a bucket into which I can put ideas and which will eventually become full up. It is the sluice gate or mill wheel through which all the ideas in the world may flow. Nothing I create is created from nothing. I am nothing but a living modification of infinite Nature, and the more I engage with Nature, physically and intellectually, the more I am alive.

The more we follow the interpretative, or hermeneutical, circle, the deeper becomes our understanding of Iota. The deeper our understanding of Iota, the greater our psychological and physical integrity, and the higher we ascend on the spiral staircase towards peace of mind and happiness.

*Humanist existentialism and the Iotic attitude.* To adopt the Iotic attitude is to accept the principle that your existence is all that you have. You don't rely on, appeal to, or blame external agents. You seek no emotional refuge. You take responsibility for your actions. You are not devious. You mean what you say and you say what you mean. You act positively and honestly. You do not indulge in any sort of blackmail – emotional, moral, religious or criminal. You don't align yourself with secretive societies, conspiracies or plots. You treat others as equals and as ends in themselves rather than as a means to an end. Wherever and whenever there is a choice between your humanity and anything else – job, religion, career or politics – you put humanity first. You do not say things about other people that you would not be prepared to say to their face. You do not blame; you do not 'name and shame'. Such values apply to government as well as to the individual.

*Heidegger's choice.* The choice Heidegger said we are continually making as human beings is not one between two courses of action but between choosing and not choosing. He tells us that to fail to choose is to fail – period. We can choose and win, says Heidegger, or we can lose and try to *appear* to win. This is essentially the same distinction that Plato makes between the chained prisoners in the cave and the person who leaves the cave and makes his way out into the daylight. When he comes back into the cave, he appears to the prisoners to be a crazy loser and they congratulate each other on their appearance of having won. But the real losers are those who are held captive by their laziness, their obsession with outward appearance and their willingness to let others dictate to them what they should think and believe about the shadows dancing on the wall.

*Beware of the sloth.* Failure as a person, as opposed to failure in one's career or to make money or become famous, is always caused by that person's laziness, whether physical or intellectual. It is intellectual laziness to allow someone else to think for you, or to expect other people to do for you what you can do for yourself. Laziness leads to self-indulgence; self-indulgence leads to obesity, alcoholism and drug-dependency. The lazier I am today, the lazier I shall be tomorrow, and the more difficult it will be to break out of my vicious circle of laziness and the febrile self-justification that goes with it.

The abdication of reason associated with willingness to believe unquestioningly leads, at best, to a sense of dissatisfaction towards the end of one's life, and at worse to deep regret that had you had the courage and energy you might have done things differently. To pray that the Virgin Mary will pray for you at the hour of your death is the height of passivity and intellectual laziness.

*Simple rules for living.* Treat every day as if it might be the last in your life, while at the same time believing that you will live to see the consequences of all your actions. Get up early in the morning. Engage with life. Post your own letters. Have children. Don't follow the crowd. Work hard. Deceive no one, least of all yourself. Widen your interests. Take your nose out of the Bible, the Talmud or the Qu'ran. Get up off your knees. Take risks. Seize the day. Fear no one. Look up! Reach up! Higher! Higher still!

Love; laugh; live.

*Rats on a raft.* We are like rats on a storm-tossed raft. The majority, fearful of disaster, rush from side to side as the raft tips with each passing wave. Only a few see that they are safer not follow the crowd but to keep in balance with the motion of the raft and the raging of the sea.

*The reins of responsibility.* Sartre's example of indecision is that of the son of a Nazi collaborator during World War II who can't make up his mind whether to stay at home and look after his ailing mother, or join the resistance movement and fight the Nazis. He goes to Sartre and asks what he should do. But of course, he has *already* chosen what to do. He has chosen not to make up his own mind but to ask someone else to make it up for him. He has, by his actions, turned himself into a ditherer, a man of inaction who wants to hand over the reins of responsibility for his actions to someone else.

*The consequences of diotic behavior.* People who adopt the diotic attitude – those who fail to take responsibility for their lives and who blame their misfortune and lack of success on external agents – can be easily recognized. Like the prisoners in Plato's cave, they talk about illusions rather than reality. They are taken in by rhetoric, propaganda and spin. In abandoning reason, they submit themselves to a species of tyranny. They slavishly follow fashion, buy the products advertisements tell them to buy, believe every latest theory about diet and health, shop at the stores, drive the cars and buy the products they believe will foster an image that is said to be hip, cool or funky.

The more we fail to take responsibility for our actions, the deeper we sink into diotic behavior and the more freedom of action we lose – in the same way that the more a person indulges herself by overeating, the further she sinks into obesity and the more physical mobility she loses.

*Angst.* There is a price to be paid for the diotic attitude. In amongst all the glamour, glitter and appearance of success, we experience moments of anxiety about what matters: life, death, happiness, reality.

From time to time, when a glimpse of reality breaks through the thin crust of inauthenticity, we experience a sense of the futility of our existence. Absorbed for most of the time in the modern world of technology and the scramble for wealth and success, we are occasionally visited by a sudden awareness that, lurking just beyond our view is a huge, dark, and frightening world of reality. Joseph Conrad's novelette *Heart of Darkness* vividly depicts this feeling, which is expressed by one of the characters when he exclaims, 'The horror! The horror!'

*Death.* Nothing concentrates the mind so effectively as death, and when we experience a life-threatening illness or the death of someone close to us, we are sometimes confronted by a feeling of the futility of life. Such moments provide little windows into Iota – opportunities to re-orientate ourselves, stop being slaves to appearance, and start choosing to live authentically. In this way, the death of someone near to us can be regarded positively, as it provides a way of escaping from the world of appearances and embracing reality. We find ourselves again. We start making our own values rather than letting journalists, broadcasters, salesmen, politicians, spin doctors, rabbis, priests, television advertisements, gurus or peer pressure make them for us. We stop having to run on the Wheel of Ixion in order to keep our balance. We start running in balance, of our own volition, for the joy of running.

*Euthanasia and suicide.* Suicide and euthanasia are frowned on principally for religious reasons, because the act constitutes a denial of religious teaching about the survival of an individual soul after death. Suicide is widely regarded as a shameful, cowardly, anti-social act of selfishness. But in many cases, suicide is a selfless, courageous act. Many old people who have lost the ability to look after themselves and are kept alive by medication and nursing would prefer to die than continue with a life that has turned into a burden to all concerned. But in most Western countries they are not allowed to. While a physically and mentally fit woman in her twenties can do away with her unborn child if she feels that motherhood will interfere with her career as a journalist, lawyer or television producer, an old man of seventy with motor neuron disease is obliged to endure total paralysis, incontinence, drooling and loss of speech until the lucky day he catches pneumonia and his life support system is switched off.

*The Christian gospel.* One has to be gullible, simple, fearful or all three to believe the Christian gospel. According to evangelists, the gospel message is 'good news' because it promises eternal bliss to those who accept Jesus as their Lord and Savior. The downside is that if you consciously and deliberately refuse to abdicate your powers of reason and embrace its contradictions, you will burn in hell for all eternity.

*Religion and fear.* From time immemorial, religious leaders have used fear of eternal punishment together with fascination with things that are miraculous, mysterious or secret to oblige people to live and behave in ways that are said to be pleasing to the gods (or God).

*Spinoza on miracles.* Spinoza argued that we cannot gain understanding of anything at all by means of miracles, but only through 'the fixed and immutable order of nature' – in other words, science:

[...] we know that nothing either agrees with or is contrary to nature, unless it agrees with or is contrary to these primary ideas; wherefore if we would conceive that anything could be done in nature by any power whatsoever, which would be contrary to the laws of nature, it would also be contrary to primary ideas, and we should have either to reject it is absurd, or else to cast doubt (as just shown) on primary ideas, and consequently on the existence of God, and on everything howsoever perceived. Therefore miracles, in the sense of events that are contrary to the laws of nature, so far from demonstrating to us the existence of God, would, on the contrary, lead us to doubt it, where otherwise we might have been absolutely certain of it, as knowing that nature follows a fixed and immutable order.

Let us take miracle as meaning that which cannot be explained through natural causes. This may be interpreted in two senses: either as that which has natural causes, but cannot be examined by the human intellect; or as that which has no cause save God and God's will. But as all things which come to pass through natural causes, come to pass also solely through the will and power of God, it comes to this, that a miracle, whether it has natural causes or not, is a result which cannot be explained by its cause, that is a phenomenon which surpasses human understanding; but from such a phenomenon, and certainly from a result surpassing our understanding, we can gain no knowledge. For whatsoever we understand clearly and distinctly should be plain to us either in itself or by means of something else clearly and distinctly understood; wherefore from a miracle or a phenomenon which we cannot understand, we can gain no knowledge of God's essence, or existence, or indeed anything about God or nature; whereas, when we know that all things are ordained and ratified by God, that the operations of nature follow from the essence of God, and that the laws of nature are eternal decrees and solutions of God, we must perforce conclude that our knowledge of God and of God's will increases in proportion to our knowledge and clear understanding of nature, as we see how she depends on her primal cause, and how she works according to eternal law. Wherefore, so far as our understanding goes, those phenomena which we clearly and distinctly understand have much better right to be called the works of God, and to be referred to the will of God than those about which we are entirely ignorant, although they appeal powerfully to the imagination, and compel men's admiration.

*The Arian heresy.* Arius was a Christian bishop who became involved in a dispute with Bishop Alexander of Alexandria over whether the Son of God was consubstantial and co-eternal with God the Father. His argument was in the form of two syllogisms that revealed a fatal contradiction in the fundamental tenet of Christian doctrine:

<u>Syllogism (1)</u>
*Premise*: All begotten beings have beginning of existence.
*Premise*: Jesus Christ was the begotten son of God the Father.
*Demonstration*: Therefore, Jesus Christ had beginning of existence.

<u>Syllogism (2)</u>
*Premise*: Beings that have a beginning of existence can be neither consubstantial nor co-eternal with a being that does not have beginning of existence.
*Premise*: Jesus Christ had a beginning of existence.
*Premise*: God the Father did not have a beginning of existence.
*Demonstration*: Jesus Christ is neither consubstantial nor co-eternal with God the Father.

Arius pointed out that if the Son had a beginning of existence, there was a time when the Son 'was not', from which it necessarily followed that 'he had his substance from nothing'.

If the words 'Father', 'Son' and 'begotten' have meaning, it is impossible to avoid Arius's conclusion, and it is upon this obvious contradiction that the whole edifice of Christian doctrine is founded.

*First Council of Nicaea.* Emperor Constantine called a council of delegates, summoned from all parts of the Holy Roman Empire, to resolve the Arian controversy. With the exception of Britain, all dioceses into which the empire had been divided sent at least one representative. Pope Sylvester I, being too infirm to be present, sent two presbyters as delegates. This was the First Council of Nicaea. Twenty-two of the bishops at the council came as supporters of Arius. When passages from Arius' writings were read out they were denounced as blasphemous by the large majority of the council participants. Under the influence of Constantine, the assembled bishops agreed upon a creed – the Nicene Creed – which included the words 'consubstantial with the Father'. On June 19, 325, the council and the Emperor issued a circular letter to the churches in and around Alexandria. Arius and two supporters were deposed and exiled, and three dissenting bishops affixed their signatures in deference to the emperor.

*The Gregorian Credo.* In the late sixth century, Bishop Gregory of Tours set down a personal credo whose main purpose was to refute the Arian heresy:

> I believe in God the Father omnipotent. I believe in Jesus Christ his only Son, our Lord God, born of the Father, not created. I believe that he has always been with the Father, not only since time began but before all time. For the Father could not have been so named unless he had a son; and there could be no son without a father. But as for those who say: 'There was a time when he was not' I reject them with curses, and call men to witness that they are separated from the church. I believe that the word of the Father by which all things were made was Christ. I believe that this word was made flesh and by its suffering the world was redeemed, and I believe that humanity, not deity, was subject to the suffering. I believe that he rose again on the third day, that he freed sinful man, that he ascended to

heaven, that he sits on the right hand of the Father, that he will come to judge the living and the dead. I believe that the Holy Spirit proceeded from the Father and the Son, that it is not inferior and is not of later origin, but is God, equal and always co-eternal with the Father and the Son, consubstantial in its nature, equal in omnipotence, equally eternal in its essence, and that it has never existed apart from the Father and the Son and is not inferior to the Father and the Son. I believe that this holy Trinity exists with separation of persons, and one person is that of the Father, another that of the Son, another that of the Holy Spirit. And in this Trinity I confess that there is one Deity, one power, one essence. I believe that the blessed Mary was a virgin after the birth as she was a virgin before. I believe that the soul is immortal but that nevertheless it has no part in deity. And I faithfully believe all things that were established at Nicæa by the three hundred and eighteen bishops. But as to the end of the world I hold beliefs which I learned from our forefathers, that Antichrist will come first. An Antichrist will first propose circumcision, asserting that he is Christ; next he will place his statue in the temple at Jerusalem to be worshiped, just as we read that the Lord said: 'You shall see the abomination of desolation standing in the holy place.' But the Lord himself declared that that day is hidden from all men, saying; 'But of that day and that hour knoweth no one not even the angels in heaven, neither the Son, but the Father alone.' Moreover we shall here make answer to the heretics who attack us, asserting that the Son is inferior to the Father since he is ignorant of this day. Let them learn then that Son here is the name applied to the Christian people, of whom God says: 'I shall be to them a father and they shall be to me for sons.' For if he had spoken these words of the only-begotten Son he would never have given the angels first place. For he uses these words: 'Not even the angels in heaven nor the Son', showing that he spoke these words not of the only-begotten but of the people of adoption. But our end is Christ himself, who will graciously bestow eternal life on us if we turn to him.

Read with an open mind, the contradictions, rationalisations and incoherencies of Bishop Gregory's credo will become readily apparent.

*Authoritative theological declarations.* In saying 'I faithfully believe all things that were established at Nicæa by the three hundred and eighteen bishops', Bishop Gregory gives us an invaluable insight into how the Christian religion 'works'. He shows us that religion is founded not on reason but rather in a joint declaration, written in a language only the educated can understand, of a majority of secretive clerics who dress up in vestments and wear fancy hats.

*The Nicene Creed.* In 1546 at the Council of Trent the Nicene Creed was amended and adopted by the Roman Catholic Church as definitive of Christian belief:

> Credo in unum Deum Patrem omnipotentem; factorum coeli et terrae, visibilium

omnium et invisibilium. Et in unum Dominum Jesum Christum, Filium Dei unigenitum, et ex Patre natum ante omnia saecula, Deum de Deo, Lumen de Lumine, Deum verum de Deo vero, genitum, non factum, consubstantialem Patri; per quem omnia facta sunt; qui propter nos homines et propter nostram salutem descendit de coelis, et incarnatus est de Spiritu Sancto ex Maria virgine, et homo factus est; crucifixus etiam pro nobis sub Pontio Pilato, passus et sepultus est; et resurrexit tertia die, secundum Scripturas; et ascendit in coelum, sedet ad dexteram Patris; et iterum venturus est, cum gloria, judicare vivos et mortuos; cujus regni non erit finis. Et in Spiritum Sanctum, Dominum et vivificantem, qui ex Patre filioque procedit; qui cum Patre et Filio simul adoratur et conglorificatur; qui locutus est per Prophetas. Et unam, sanctam, catholicam et apostolicam ecclesiam. Confiteor unum baptisma in remissionem peccatorum; et expecto resurrectionem mortuorum, et vitam venturi seculi. Amen.

*or:*

I believe in one God, the Father Almighty,
Maker of heaven and earth,
And of all things visible and invisible:
And in one Lord Jesus Christ, the only-begotten Son of God,
Born of the father before time began,
God of God, Light of Light,
True God of true God,
Begotten, not made,

One in substance with the Father,
By whom all things were made;
Who for us men and for our salvation came down from heaven,
And was made flesh by the Holy Ghost of the Virgin Mary,
And was made man,
And was crucified for us under Pontius Pilate.
He suffered death and was buried,
And the third day he rose again according to the Scriptures,
And ascended into heaven,
And sitteth on the right hand of the Father.
And he shall come again with glory to judge both the living and the dead:
Whose kingdom shall have no end.
And I believe in the Holy Ghost,
The Lord and giver of life,
Who proceedeth from the Father and the Son,
Who with the Father and the Son is adored and glorified,
Who spoke through the Prophets.
And I believe in one Catholic and Apostolic Church.
I acknowledge one Baptism for the remission of sins.
And I look for the Resurrection of the dead,
And the life of the world to come.
Amen.

Week after week, serious, intelligent people recite these words without reflecting upon what they claim to believe.

*Faith and power.* Wherever faith is said to exist it can always be traced back to man-made declarations backed up by threats of exclusion or punishment in this world or the next. In this way, the Christian church has, down the ages, assimilated power to itself and used that power to bring people into subjection through fear of exclusion or punishment in an afterlife in which they have been induced to believe – by means of threats of exclusion or punishment!

*Blasphemy.* Accusation of 'blasphemy' is the only refuge available to the theologian or religious person who is unable to find a rational reply when confronted with the contradictions of Christian doctrine. The word sends a shiver down the spine of believers, and conjures up dark images and fearful mediaeval connotations. 'Blasphemy, blasphemy!' they cry – to which the rationalist replies, unexcitedly, 'Reason, reason.'

*The Roman Catholic Church and the Mafia.* The Italian Mafia finds its roots in the remnants of the Roman bureaucracy that was disempowered after the fall of Rome. Its ruthless practice of making offers that cannot be refused is no different, essentially, from the Roman Catholic Church's threat of eternal punishment for those who break its rules. Each organization makes money and assimilates temporal power by inculcating collective fear. Few, if any, priests have ever dared to name members of the Mafia, as to do so would be to break the confidentiality of the confessional. In that refusal they turn themselves into accessories to crimes against humanity. We should not be shocked or surprised at this: humanity always takes second place to religion.

*Nietzsche on Christianity:*

> When we hear the old bells ringing out on a Sunday morning, we ask ourselves: can it be possible? This for a Jew, crucified 2000 years ago, who said he was the son of God. The proof for such a claim is wanting. Within our times the Christian religion is surely an antiquity jutting out from a far-distant olden time; and the fact that people believe such a claim (while they are otherwise so strict in testing assertions) is perhaps the oldest part of this heritage. A god who conceives children with a mortal woman; a wise man who calls upon us to work no more, to judge no more, but to heed the signs of the imminent apocalypse; the justice that accepts the innocent man as a proxy sacrifice; someone who has his disciples drink his blood; prayers for miraculous interventions; sins against a god, atoned for by a god; fear of the afterlife, to which death is the gate; the figure of the cross as a symbol, in a time that no longer knows the purpose and shame of the cross – how horridly all this wafts over us, as from the grave of the ancient past! Are we to believe that such things are still believed?

*Reason and scripture.* Should scripture be made to agree with reason, or should reason be made to agree with the teaching of scripture? This is a particularly difficult question for religious people to answer because if they tamper with reason they cut the ground from beneath their feet and abdicate their ability to say anything that has meaning, while if they tamper with the meaning of scripture they call in question its validity, upon which they rely to support the beliefs that they profess.

If we are to live honestly and in good faith, we have to make a choice between rejecting unreserved belief in the Bible in favor of reason, or suspending reason in favor of unreserved belief in the Bible. If the latter position is taken up, we cannot legitimately present rational arguments for belief in miracles, creationism or intelligent design; if the former, then all we can do is regard the contents of the Bible or the Qu'ran in the same sort of way as we regard the works of Homer and Hesiod: as myths and legends that may be useful for moral guidance but contribute nothing to our knowledge of matters of fact or existence.

To sum up, theology is incompatible with any discipline that demands rational argument or logical deduction.

*Abraham's problem.* In *Fear and Trembling*, Kierkegaard analyses the problem that confronted Abraham when God commanded him to take his only son Isaac up to a mountain and sacrifice him as a burnt offering. Isaac had been conceived when his mother Sarah was over ninety, and God had promised Abraham that Isaac would be the founding father of his chosen people. Abraham had already displayed faith in believing that God would allow Sarah to conceive so late in life. Now, he was faced with what appeared to be an impossible dilemma. Not only was he being commanded by God to do something that was forbidden by Mosaic Law (make a human sacrifice), but he was also being commanded to kill his son, without whom the great nation which God had promised would never come into being. Nor was Abraham free to discuss the dilemma with any other person: he was obliged to tell no one of it and to keep secret what God had commanded him to do.

*The tragic hero.* Kierkegaard makes a contrast between Abraham's dilemma and that of the tragic hero. The tragic hero, he says, is faced with a decision that is within the ethical norms of society. An example might be the choice between separating Siamese twins to save one life out of two, or obeying the parents' wish not to separate them and so allowing both to die. In such a case, whichever decision is taken by the hero can be justified on the grounds that it accords with at least one of the ethical norms of society, what Kierkegaard refers to as the 'universal'. This is not so in Abraham's case. He cannot be heroic and conform to what society regards as ethical. He either obeys God (the absolute) and disobeys society, or obeys society (the universal) and disobeys God. Unlike the tragic hero, Abraham can never at a later date explain why he acted as he did or justify his actions in terms that society will judge to be ethical.

The genuine tragic hero, Kierkegaard says, sacrifices himself and everything he has for the universal: his action, every emotion in him belongs to the universal, he is revealed, and in his disclosure he is the beloved son of ethics. This cannot apply in Abraham's case. He does nothing for the universal and keeps the whole thing secret.

A paradox results: either the individual stands in an absolute relation to God, in which case the ethical norms of society are not the highest, or Abraham is no sort of hero in the conventionally accepted sense. In this way a fundamental conflict between the normative ethics of a society and the absolute commands of God is revealed.

*Religion versus humanity.* Kierkegaard's discussion of the tragic hero reveals an important fact about the consequences of belief in a God whose divine commands overrule the ethical norms of society. What Kierkegaard is saying is what is implicit in religious belief: that whenever there is a conflict between religion and humanity, religion must always come first.

*The strength of the absurd.* Kierkegaard tells us that the only way Abraham can resolve the conflict between God's command and the requirements of the Mosaic Law is by making a leap of faith on the strength of the absurd. He has to shut his eyes to the law which forbids human sacrifice – which was given to Moses by God in the first place – and have faith in the absurd supposition that the God he worships can break the laws he lays down as and when he chooses.

There is no getting away from the conclusion Kierkegaard reaches: spiritual faith is possible only by abdicating not only human reason, but by subjugating commonsense humanity to religious absurdity.

*Absurdity heaped upon absurdity.* Members of absolutist religions have to make three leaps of faith, each on the basis of absurdity. First, they have to have faith in the person who teaches them to believe in the existence of an absolute God who stands outside nature; second, they have to make believe that they can converse directly with that supposed being (or that someone can do so on their behalf) – and finally, they have to abdicate their rational powers in order to believe the stories and observe the ordinances taught them by religious leaders who claim to have a superior ability to interpret Scripture.

*The Christian dilemma.* Christians are caught in an awful dilemma. If they depend upon religious authority to dictate to them what to believe and what not to believe, they have to cast aside all thoughts of independent, rational thought. Either they have to do what they are told and accept without question the doctrines and ordinances of their religion; or, if they rely on the Holy Spirit to 'guide them into all truth' they assume a position of spiritual superiority that cuts them off from other Christians. Whichever they choose, they are obliged to suppress the natural light of reason and pretend to be something they are not and can never be. Such pretence of spiritual superiority contradicts the Iotic principle and always results in conflict of some sort.

*The Waco massacre.* Belief in a God whose authority transcends human ethics encourages people in power to believe that they have a direct line to God and are commanded by him to do his will. This belief can have very dangerous consequences.

On February 28 1993, the United States Bureau of Alcohol, Tobacco and Firearms attempted to execute a search warrant at the Davidian ranch at Mount Carmel, a property near Waco, Texas. An exchange of gunfire resulted in the deaths of four agents and six Davidians. A fifty day siege by the Federal Bureau of Investigation ended when fire destroyed the compound. Seventy-six people, including 21 children, two pregnant women and the cult leader Vernon Wayne Howell, died in the fire.

The Branch Davidians were originally Seventh-day Adventists, a fundamentalist sect that emerged in the 19$^{th}$ century. Two important doctrines provided the core beliefs of the Branch Davidians: a preoccupation with eschatology, and a conviction that its doctrine was the only valid one. In 1929, excommunicated Seventh-day Adventist Victor Houteff established his own following in California. In 1935 he moved with his disciples to Texas and named their compound Mount Carmel, claiming he was God's messenger. Houteff styled himself as a prophet. He called his church The Shepherd's Rod Seventh-day Adventists, but in 1942 changed the name to the Davidian Seventh-day Adventists Association in order to emphasize his belief that he was the Old Testament King David.

After Houteff's death, his wife took over the leadership of the cult and predicted that God's judgment would begin on April 22, 1959. When her prophecy failed, the group splintered. Many became disillusioned; others formed their own factions.

The largest faction remained near Mount Carmel and was led by Benjamin Roden, who changed the group's name to the Branch Davidians. Roden proclaimed himself a 'chosen vessel of God' bearing the message of the fifth angel in the Book of Revelation. At his death, his wife Lois assumed the leadership, claiming to carry the message of the sixth angel.

In 1981 Vernon Howell joined the Branch Davidians as Lois's 'handyman'. When Lois died in 1986, a skirmish ensued between Howell and Lois's son, George, over leadership. At stake were control of the cult, and the claim of divine anointing as a prophet.

By 1988 Howell had gained control of the cult and its compound at Mount Carmel. In the ensuing two years he recruited followers from across the United States and several other countries. He enticed pubescent girls into becoming his sexual partners by naming them as 'wives' and declaring that they had been chosen by God to help him repopulate planet earth. He manipulated his followers in virtually every dimension of their lives, including sleep, prayer, Bible study, diet, reading, music, and finances.

Howell changed his name to Koresh. There was a reason for the change. He believed himself to be Jesus Christ, and that he had been anointed by God to reconstruct the perfect human family and restore the world to God's rule. He used his name as an acronym for the doctrines he imposed on his followers:

K = King James. Koresh taught that the King James Version of the Bible was the only acceptable translation of Scripture.

O = Obedience. Koresh pressured his followers into surrendering their ability to think and question independently. Techniques used by Koresh included emphasizing God's vengeance against those who left the cult, extending to members a counterfeit sense of love and belonging, leading members to believe that his will was God's will, and indoctrinating members with a siege mentality designed to alienate them from the rest of the world.

R = Reincarnation and Return of Christ. Howell proclaimed himself to be the reincarnation of Jesus Christ and the fulfilment of Christ's second coming.

E = Esoteric Biblical interpretations. Koresh claimed to be the Lamb of Revelation Chap. 5. In the process of interpreting Scripture, he ignored language, context, history and doctrine. In their place he substituted personal revelations, disjointed arguments and mystical symbolism.

S = Sex. Koresh used sex to control his followers. He coerced men to surrender their wives to him for his sexual enjoyment. He regarded prepubescent girls as fair game. He claimed that God had revealed to him that he could have sex with any woman he wanted.

H = Holy Spirit. Koresh claimed that his power and inspiration came from the Holy Spirit. He taught that the Mother of the godhead is the Holy Spirit and the daughter of the godhead is the Holy Ghost who would be incarnated as Koresh's eternal mate.

*The common ground that absolutist religions share with Koresh.* The vast majority of religious people look on the Branch Davidian cult in utter disdain, claiming that the beliefs of that cult have nothing whatsoever to do with their own. But closer examination of the KORESH mnemonic reveals that the methods used by David Koresh to subjugate the members of his flock are little different from those used down the centuries by many religions. In the case of Islam, Judaism and Christianity, each dictates to its members which Scriptures they may rely on as being authentic and which are to be rejected. Each uses mental and physical manipulation to pressurize followers into obedience and into surrendering their freedom to think and question independently. Each looks forward to the return or advent of a legendary Savior, Mahdi or Messiah. Each indulges in more or less esoteric hermeneutical interpretations. Each uses matters of sex and sexual prohibition as ways to control their followers, particularly women and girls.

Ultimately, there is little difference between David Koresh's claims to be party to divine revelation and Abraham's belief that he had been ordered by God to sacrifice his son, the Pope's claim to be Christ's infallible representative on earth, or the belief of a Shi'ite imam or Sunni mullah that he is doing Allah's will by sending young people to their deaths as suicide bombers.

*Universal application of the Iotic principle.* The practices, teachings and ordinances of any religion or organization are good only insofar as they cohere with the Iotic principle that if we hurt others we hurt ourselves. Wherever and whenever that principle is contravened by the leaders of any organization, political party or religion, the good name and credibility of that group is damaged. Every act of violence, torture or physical abuse damages the perpetrator in a way that can never, ever be repaired. If religious leaders (and leaders who are religious) could only grasp the simple proposition that to harm another nation is to harm one's own, then perhaps there might be hope for peace in the world.

*The single guiding principle.* Denial of the possibility of 'what is not' or 'nothingness' necessitates acceptance of the view that we are all one and, by reason of that fact, we have to reject the view that an absolute deity exists whose voice it is possible to hear or whose will it is possible to follow, and that any attempt by any human being to instruct another human being in what God wants or commands is bogus.

*Theological positivism.* Belief in an absolute God necessitates adopting a species of logical positivism. But it is a double positivism. To believe in an absolute God we have first to believe, with Descartes, that we can stand outside reality and describe it – and in describing it to assert that the God we believe in also stands outside his creation and all his creatures, including us. We might call this double positivism 'theological positivism'.

*Impossibility of mind-independent reality.* The contradiction at the heart of positivism is comparable to the contradiction at the heart of substance pluralism, for if there is a mind-independent reality, then mind and reality (or God and Nature) must be separate, and if they are separate they must be separated by something that has to exist if they are separate but that cannot exist if mind and reality (or God and Nature) are all that there is. As in the case of substance pluralism, we find ourselves disobeying Parmenides by making the assumption that things are separated by nothingness, 'that which is not' – nothing at all.

*Wittgenstein's rejection of logical positivism.* Wittgenstein starts his *Tractatus Logico-Philosophicus* by asserting that the world is all that is the case, and that the world is a totality of facts, not things. But he ends it by saying that there are things of which we cannot speak and must pass over in silence. Thus the ending effectively contradicts the beginning. It turns out that the world is not after all the totality of facts, because our *qualia* of human thoughts and feelings are inexpressible as facts. We are being told to remain silent about ideas we think about constantly but which, according to Wittgenstein, we are unable to talk about in language. The world cannot, after all, be teased out in terms of logical propositions.

What has happened here? Answer: Wittgenstein has, in the process of writing the *Tractatus*, moved away from logical positivism into what might be called structuralism. This, probably, is what he means when he refers to climbing up a ladder and, having done so, pushing it away as being of no further use.

*Showing and saying.* Wittgenstein pointed out that all philosophical theorizing is worthless and that the only meaningful way of doing philosophy is by *showing* rather than *saying*. This view echoes the existentialist dictum that we become what we are by doing what we do. On that basis, the only way to become a philosopher is to *be* a philosopher, which is to say, to love truth and live in accordance with reason.

*Reification of abstracts.* When we ask questions like 'what *is* truth?' 'what *is* justice?' or 'what *is* beauty?' we try to turn truth, justice and beauty into substantive objects and in doing so make what Wittgenstein calls a grammatical mistake. As a result, we end up in a confusion of conflicting arguments.

In particular, how can any proposition be logically legitimate that purports to refer to an object which I cannot perceive as an object? If I say '*the* pain is in my elbow' I make use of one of Bertrand Russell's definite descriptions, and as soon as I do that my use of the singular term '*the* pain' turns my pain into a substantive object and commits me to believing in the existence of at least one pain and not more than one pain which is inside *me*.

Wittgenstein argues that we cannot turn Frege's telescope back on ourselves to refer to what is going on in our own minds or the feelings of pain or hope or love that we experience. Such feelings are not 'out there' in the external world like the moon or Everest or George Washington. Our grammatical use of 'the pain' turns it into some sort of *private* object that I seem to be referring to by my use of *public* language.

But *how* do I refer to it? I can't look for this pain outside myself, so I have to try to turn Frege's telescope back on myself in an attempt to examine what is going on inside me. I have to make use of introspection. This is what Descartes tries to do in his *Meditations*. He shuts out the world and tries to think about what is going on inside his own mind. But his belief that this is possible rests on his prior belief that mind and matter are separate – which lands him back in the contradiction implicit in supposing two substances that are entirely separate and yet separated by nothing.

Over and over again the supposition that there can be more than one substance leads us into contradiction. This has particular application when the doctrine of transubstantiation, turning the bread and wine into the body and blood of Jesus Christ, is considered.

*God in three persons.* The Christian doctrine of the Holy Trinity, which holds that the godhead is three persons in one, Father, Son and Holy Ghost, is a further example of theological contradiction. It prompts a question about personal identity to which no coherent answer can be given if one attempts to do so from a dualistic point of view.

*Personal identity.* What is personal identity? Is it identity of substance? No. Is it identity of the body? No. Is it identity of the human being? No. Then what? Here is John Locke's answer:

> This being premised, to find wherein *personal identity* consists, we must consider what *person* stands for; which, I think, is a thinking intelligent being that has reason and reflection and can consider itself as itself, the same thinking thing in different times and places; which it does only by that consciousness which is inseparable from thinking and, as it seems to me, essential to

it: it being impossible for anyone to perceive without perceiving that he does perceive. When we see, hear, smell, taste, feel, meditate or will anything, we know that we do so. [...] For since consciousness always accompanies thinking, and it is that that makes everyone to be what he calls self, and thereby distinguishes himself from all other thinking things: in this alone consists *personal identity*, i.e. the sameness of a rational being. And as far as consciousness can be extended backwards to any past action or thought, so far reaches the identity of that person: it is the same *self* now it was then, and it is the same *self* with this present one that now reflects on it, that that action was done.

Locke seems to be suggesting that personal identity consists in the chain of past memories of an individual rational being. But this throws up a serious problem. Because no real distinction can be made between an individual rational being and a person, Locke is effectively putting the same expression on either side of an equals sign. He is saying that a person's identity is to be found in that *same* person's memories. As a result, the theory is vulnerable to *reductio ad absurdam*. We might paraphrase it by saying that a person's personal identity depends on that person having a chain of remembered events and on being able to identify them as belonging to the same, or identical, person who experienced them as the person who is now remembering them.

By suggesting that it is impossible for anyone to perceive without perceiving, Locke seems to imply that the human mind can be split in two, one part perceiving, the other part perceiving that the first is perceiving.

Locke is one of those philosophers who Wittgenstein likens to someone trying to get out of a room by pushing on a locked door. He needs to be turned round and shown the open exit behind him. That exit is the relinquishment of substance pluralism and belief in the existence of absolutely individual persons, and acceptance that every human being is a temporary mode of nature which, on death, slips back into the infinite and eternal mind.

*Impossibility of absolute identity.* When we judge a thing to change and yet remain the same, we do so because we experience that change or persistence relative to ourselves. Our willingness to ascribe change and identity to things is dependent on the apparent change or lack of change in things that we perceive with the senses, whether directly or by means of manufactured equipment like telescopes or microscopes. All arguments aimed at justifying belief in the *absolute* identity of objects, persons or artifacts are bound, ultimately, to fall into contradiction.

*World without beginning.* We can confidently forecast that however many blackboards are covered in however much chalk, it will never be proved that the universe had a beginning, for the simple reason that what we know as the physical universe is only one of the infinite and eternal attributes of Iota.

Just because *we* see finite existence in terms of a beginning and an end does not mean to say that infinite existence has a beginning or an end. In fact, such a thought is a conceptual impossibility.

*Finite but unbounded.* Some theorists claim that the cosmos is finite but unbounded. They might equally say that it is bounded but infinite. Either way, the statement is a contradiction in terms, as a boundary implies finitude and infinity implies what is unbounded.

Ultimately, human language breaks down when it tries to describe Iota. As finite modes of Iota, we are capable only of describing, from within, what appears to us to be finite. Any attempt on our part to describe Iota in a positivistic way, as if from without, is futile. Because it is infinite, Iota is only asymptotically describable.

*The expanding universe.* Because we are unable to step outside reality and view it with absolute objectivity, the theory that the universe is expanding cannot be absolutely reliable, as that expansion is seen by us relatively rather than absolutely. Our language as well as our mathematics breaks down when we try to describe such a concept, for by 'expanding' we mean 'getting bigger than it was in the past' – but there is no 'past', and Iota, being in every way infinite, cannot 'get bigger'.

If a clock can appear to run slower to an observer traveling at or near the speed of light relative to the clock, why should not galaxies appear to be getting further apart from each other as a result of forces that are unknown to us?

*Back to basics.* As soon as we talk about the beginning of the universe, we have to talk about the cause of that beginning. In doing so, we tacitly assent to the belief in a first cause that sets everything going. Belief in such a first cause necessitates belief in something existing before our supposed beginning of existence. That is a contradiction: an absolute beginning is not an absolute beginning if something pre-exists it. And so we find ourselves back in the position of believing in a creator. If we then ask ourselves about the nature of such a creator, we can only assume that it is self-causing – otherwise we would find ourselves in an infinite regress. So we now believe in an infinitely powerful, self-causing creator. But out of what does the universe come? We can only answer that it comes from the infinite self-causing creator. So now we believe in a self causing and self-perpetuating creator that is identical with its creation – in other words, Iota.

*The forbidden question.* Even if some mathematician or physicist in the future were to convince herself and us that she had found the beginning of everything, the project of science would then be burdened with an impossible task, namely to discover what caused that beginning and – more importantly – the reason why it caused it.

This was the question that the Pope did not want Stephen Hawking to address. In forbidding Hawking to make such an enquiry, the Pope made a veiled threat to science, aware as he was that pursuance of the question, 'What happened before the Big Bang?' must inevitably lead to a rejection of belief in a creator or designer who stands absolutely apart from the universe.

Eternity cannot be one-ended. If something has a beginning its existence cannot be eternal. But Iota is eternal. It is infinite in infinite ways and is its own cause.

*Science, theology and faith.* For physicists, belief in the Big Bang is based on faith in the reliability of mathematics; for non-physicists belief in the Big Bang is based on the reliability of physicists. In a similar way, theologians' belief in God is based on faith in the reliability of Scripture, while for those who cannot or do not wish to enter into the toil of hermeneutical interpretation, belief in God is based on faith in those who have interpreted scripture for them and taught them what to believe. The great difference between science and religion is that science encourages open-minded research and scepticism, while religions prohibit both, using fear of the supernatural to promote faith in logical contradictions.

*The defeat of absolutism.* Zeno's paradoxes are a subtle way of reducing to absurdity the supposition that space, time and simultaneity are absolute. The cause of these paradoxes is the belief that entities can be separated by empty space. The only way to escape them is to stop viewing the marching soldiers, Achilles, the tortoise or the arrow as occupying indivisible points in space, and to start looking upon them as parts of a relative coordinate system in which there are no gaps. Once we can look at space-time in this way, it is easy to see that Achilles, the marching soldiers or the arrow are *already* in motion relative to an infinite number of coordinate systems; and the absurdity of the notion that, in order to move Achilles must somehow reach points that are absolutely fixed, absolutely separate and absolutely motionless in space becomes readily apparent.

Just as it is impossible for points in space to be separated by nothingness, so is it impossible for a supposed supernatural being to be separated from 'his' supposed creation, or for absolutely nothing to exist before a supposed Big Bang.

*Possibilism and counterfactual worlds.* In what way can the proposition, 'Had Monica Lewinsky never been an intern at the White House, George W. Bush might never have become President of the United States of America' be said to be true? The logician's solution is to introduce the concepts of possibility and necessity to make statements about counterfactual worlds in the form, 'Possibly, if Monica Lewinsky is not an intern at the White House, George W. Bush does not become President.'

Possibilists take matters a step further by re-wording the same modal inference as 'A possible world exists in which Monica Lewinsky does not work at the White House and George W. Bush does not become President.' The philosopher David Lewis went so far as to argue that counterfactual worlds are not merely possible but that they *necessarily* exist.

We always land in trouble when we speak of 'what is not', and the attempt to form logical propositions about worlds that do not actually exist lands us in a particularly tight spot when it comes to applying names to counterfactual people, places, or things.

If we suppose counterfactual worlds in which Everest *is not* a mountain, Hollywood *is not* where they make films, or Adolph Hitler *did not* order the invasion of Poland in 1939, names and naming expressions that we use to describe the real world cease to make sense. Some or all of their connotations are lost or become contradictory, and we start living, as James Thurber put it, in the pluperfect subjunctive. We have to return to John Stuart Mill's idea that names act simply as identification tags that mean as little to us as the luggage labels mean to baggage handlers at Kennedy Airport – and don't ask *why* the airport is called Kennedy. If we are to believe the possibilists there are worlds that actually exist in which the man after whom Kennedy Airport was named was not assassinated and was not called Kennedy. As the saying goes, if your uncle had been your aunt, the world would have been a very different place.

*Might-have-been worlds.* Continually reflecting on what might have been 'if only things had been different' weakens the resolve and puts a brake on living life to the full. The more we conduct our lives rationally and positively today, the less reason we shall have for remorse or regret tomorrow. Even if, when tomorrow comes, we have cause for regret, that regret changes nothing: all it does is to weaken us further and hinder our ability to put what is past behind us. By being sorry for ourselves we invite others to be sorry for us and make ourselves a burden on society.

*Parallel universes.* Observable subatomic particles are said to constitute, collectively, the physical universe, by which is meant the whole of physical reality – what Descartes might call extension. However, experiments indicate that photons interfere with one another in such a way that suggests the existence of unobservable 'shadow' subatomic particles. Although we cannot see or detect these subatomic shadow particles, their existence is inferred from the patterns of light, penumbra and darkness that result when a beam of light is shone through one of two narrow slits. From this, it is inferred by some quantum physicists that shadow universes, or possible worlds composed of unobservable shadow particles, necessarily exist.

To quote the physicist David Deutsch: 'we might think of calling the shadow particles, collectively, a parallel universe, for they too are affected by tangible particles only through interference phenomena. But we can do better than that. For it turns out that shadow particles are partitioned among themselves in exactly the same way as the universe of tangible particles is partitioned from them. In other words, they do not form a single, homogenous parallel universe vastly larger than the tangible one, but rather a huge number of parallel universes, each similar in composition to the tangible one, and each obeying the same laws of physics, but differing in that the particles are in different positions in each universe.'

Because we understand David Deutsch to be a quantum physicist at the University of Oxford, we have faith in his scientific method and the validity of his statements about observation of photon behavior. If, as a result of reading his book *The Fabric of Reality*, we are to believe in parallel universes, we can only do so on the basis of a prior belief in his authority as a scientist. That does not prevent us from critically and sceptically examining what he has written. For example, when he writes: 'it turns out that shadow particles are partitioned among themselves in exactly the same way as the universe of tangible particles is partitioned from them,' we have to take his word for it that it turns out this way, and that he somehow knows with absolute certainty that shadow particles are partitioned in *exactly* the same way as tangible particles. The same applies to his assertion about the existence and nature of parallel universes.

*Willingness to believe experts.* There is a tendency, common among those who are interested in science and theology, to believe statements like those of David Deutsch without question. It is easier and more pleasant to bask in the reflected glory of an eminent scientist or theologian than to read what he says critically and sceptically.

Even the most erudite scientists are human. The publication of books promoting an exciting new theory heightens one's standing in the scientific community, is financially profitable and is good for self esteem. But at least when we make our leap of faith to believe in parallel universes, we do so on the basis of a rational judgment about documented scientific experiments and findings, which, by and large, are accepted – or at least not ridiculed – by the scientific community. No such rational basis is available to support religious belief. If we try to interpret the Scriptures for ourselves, we find inconsistency and contradiction; if we rely on theologians, our faith is not in God but in those whose works and sermons rely entirely on hermeneutical interpretation and arguments of persuasion.

*Faith in theologians.* A doctorate in theology goes a long way when it comes to persuading an audience or readership (particularly a Christian audience or readership) that is hungry for spiritual guidance or reassurance, and the fact that one has attended an eminent theologian's lecture or read his book is undoubtedly good for some people's self-esteem. But belief in God can never be justified by science, nor can religious faith be based on reason. No experiment in the world will ever prove the existence of a god who stands outside Nature, for the simple reason that all scientific experimentation and hypothetical deduction takes place within Nature and is based on natural laws, while, by definition, the creator or designer God stands outside nature and is supposed to be supernatural. This applies whether we take the deist view of a God who withdraws and lets the universe run on as a perfect machine, or the theist view of a God who intervenes in human affairs by answering prayers and working miracles.

*Using Scripture to support a scientific theory.* In 1901 David Wardlaw Scott published *Terra Firma: the Earth not a planet, proved from Scripture, reason, and fact.* The book is larded heavily with biblical references, which the author uses to support his view that the world is flat, founded on water and motionless in space. In his concluding remarks he writes: 'Of one thing I am perfectly certain, namely, that I have proved that the Earth is not a planet, and all the astronomers of Christendom will never be able to overthrow that fact. I confess that at times I have felt sad that the stability of the Earth should ever have required proving at all, as such shows into what a low condition sin has brought the erring intellect of man.'

*Using scientific theories in support of theology.* In his book *God's Undertaker: has science buried God?* John Lennox attempts to show that science 'points towards' the existence of intelligent design. It is a work flawed by the fact that the author selects theories which he believes support his argument but omits those that do not. As a committed Christian, Lennox cannot possess what every scientist and philosopher must possess: a completely open mind. His religious belief is the ball and chain which holds him back from addressing his own question without situating the appreciation of the problem he has set himself.

*Science: the ladder with no top step.* Scientists do not set out to 'bury' any idea: what they do is to use observation, experiment, hypothetical deduction and more experiment and more observation to climb, step by step, up the infinitely tall ladder of knowledge. As time passes, scientific theories that were once held to be sacrosanct have to be abandoned – obvious examples being the abandonment of belief in geocentricity, and the existence of phlogiston and ether.

By contrast, theologians are concerned with the interpretation of ancient texts, commentaries on those texts and interpretation of those commentaries. When scientists disagree over a hypothesis, the disagreement can only be resolved as a result of empirical proof; but when theologians disagree over a matter of faith, their disagreement can never be resolved, with the result that a schism results and a new sect or religion is formed.

*The great divide.* Science is concerned with matters of fact, and with the understanding and explanation of Nature as a result of observation and experiment. Theology is concerned with conjecture about the existence and character of a being or beings that are said to be set apart from Nature. Science is the servant of scientific method and rigorous, rational argument. Theology is the servant of hermeneutical interpretation and arguments of persuasion and emotion. Science is only possible through the practice of sound scientific method; but there is no such thing as theological method, sound or otherwise, nor is the use of contradictory arguments any bar to the claim of being a theologian.

Theology is a top step with no ladder; science is a ladder with no top step.

*Monism, flux and evolution.* The speculations of three pre-Socratic philosophers, Parmenides, Heraclitus and Anaxagoras anticipated much of what is today taken for granted by physics and evolutionary science. If we combine their speculations, a worldview that is strikingly similar to that of quantum theory emerges: the world is one (Parmenides); matter is in motion and motion is in matter (Heraclitus); everything is part of every thing, and every thing is part of everything (Anaxagoras).

Parmenides forbade us to speak of 'what is not', and pointed out that for things to be *absolutely* separate they would have to be separated by nothing at all, i.e. they would not be separate. Heraclitus denied absolute identity, saying that it is impossible to step twice into the same river. Anaxagoras deserves to be credited with being the first to propose an evolutionary theory.

*The futility of searching for origins.* The fundamental assumption the big bang theory makes is exactly the same as that made by the first verse of the book of Genesis and the first verse of St John's Gospel, namely that there was a beginning. Some physicists make a mistake when they insist that the universe had a beginning and is finite. Ignoring the fact that space-time is unified, and that the past, present and future are one, big bang theorists claim that everything 'began' at a 'point in time' many billions of years 'ago'. By assuming that there was a beginning without a cause, big bang theorists undermine the validity of their own causal theory. The only way out of the impasse is to accept that Iota is infinite, eternal, self-causing, indivisible, free, and one.

*Erasmus Darwin.* The view of Erasmus Darwin that life is all of a piece and is in a continual state of evolution finds its foundation in Spinoza's identification of God with Nature. Erasmus Darwin was a physician, scientist, physiologist, inventor and poet. He was a founder member of the Lunar Society, a group of pioneering industrialists and natural philosophers. He was a member of the Darwin-Wedgwood family, and was Charles Darwin's grandfather. His most important scientific work is *Zoönomia*. It contains a system of pathology and a treatise on generation, in which he anticipated the views of Jean-Baptiste Lamarck, widely regarded to have foreshadowed the theory of evolution. Erasmus Darwin based his theories on David Hartley's psychological theory of associationism, the essence of which is contained in the following passage from *Zoönomia*:

> Would it be too bold to imagine that, in the great length of time since the earth began to exist, perhaps millions of ages before the commencement of the history of mankind – would it be too bold to imagine that all warm-blooded animals have arisen from one living filament, which the great First Cause endued with animality, with the power of acquiring new parts, attended with new propensities, directed by irritations, sensations, volitions and associations, and thus possessing the faculty of continuing to improve by its own inherent activity, and of delivering down these improvements by generation to its posterity, world without end!

Erasmus Darwin's final poem, *The Temple of Nature*, published posthumously in 1803, was originally titled *The Origin of Society* – a title that must surely have inspired Charles Darwin when he came to titling his *The Origin of Species*. It reveals his newly-conceived theory of evolution and traces the progression of life from micro-organisms to civilized society. Erasmus Darwin anticipated much of what his grandson would later propose, apart from the idea of natural selection.

*Nietzsche on evolution*:

> Perhaps the whole human race is a temporarily limited, developmental phase of a certain species of animal, so that man evolved from the ape and will evolve back to the ape again, while no one will be there to take an interest in this strange end of the comedy. Just as with the fall of the Roman culture,

and its most important cause, the spread of Christianity, there was a general increase of loathsomeness in man within the Roman Empire, so the eventual fall of the general world culture might also cause men to be much more loathsome and finally animalistic, to the point of being apelike. Precisely because we are able to keep this perspective in mind, we might be in a position to protect the future from such an end.

*Nietzsche's mistake.* Darwin preferred to speak in terms of development rather than evolution. He discovered that some species move down as well as up the evolutionary ladder, barnacles once having evolved from something like a shrimp, and pythons having the vestiges of legs. But Nietzsche made a mistake in suggesting that we have control over our evolutionary destiny. The same sort of mistake is made by David Deutsch when he suggests that humans might at some time in the future be able to prevent the sun turning into a red giant, and was made by the British Prime Minister, Arthur Balfour, in presuming that he could assist God's purpose by helping Old Testament prophecy come true through the re-establishment of the Jews in Israel.

Nietzsche, Deutsch and Balfour exemplify the mistake made by those who believe that human beings can manipulate the universe and bring about significant change. It seems very doubtful whether attempts to save the planet or the human race will be effective.

*Emergence.* Evolutionists have difficulty explaining how intelligence came into being. The mistake they make is to think that intelligence is a 'thing' and there must have been a time when it did not exist. A common explanation is to claim that intelligence 'emerges' from matter which is unintelligent. But that is no explanation. Even if it was, no explanation is necessary: one does not have to explain how something came into being which has always existed.

Intelligence is not a 'thing'. It is an infinite and eternal attribute of Iota.

\* \* \*

### Extracts from Spinoza's *Ethics*
(The name 'God' has been replaced by 'Iota' in this section)

Part V: Of Human Freedom

6. Insofar as the mind understands all things as necessary, it has a greater power over the affects, or is less acted on by them.

Scholium: The more this knowledge that things are necessary is concerned with singular things, which we imagine more distinctly and vividly, the greater is the power of the mind over the affects, as experience itself also testifies. For we see that sadness over some good which has perished is lessened as soon as the man who has lost it realizes that this good could not, in any way, have been kept. Similarly, we see that no one pities infants because of their inability to speak, to walk, or to reason, or because they live so many years, as it were, unconscious of themselves. But if most people were born grown-up, and only one or two were born infants, then everyone would pity the infants, because they would regard infancy itself, not as a natural and necessary thing, but as a vice of nature, or a sin.

15. He who understands himself and his affects clearly and distinctly loves Iota, and does so the more, the more he understands himself and his affects.

16. This love toward Iota must engage the mind most.

17. Iota is without passions, and is not affected with any affect of joy or sadness.

18. No one can hate Iota.

19. He who loves Iota cannot strive that Iota should love him in return.

20. This love toward Iota cannot be tainted by an affect of envy or jealousy: instead, the more men we imagine to be joined to Iota by the same bond of love, the more it is encouraged.

Scholium: Similarly we can show that there is no affect which is directly contrary to this love and by which it can be destroyed. So we can conclude that this love is the most constant of all the affects, and insofar as it is related to the body, cannot be destroyed, unless it is destroyed with the body itself. What the nature of this love is insofar as it is related only to the mind, we shall see later. [...] From this it is clear that the power of the mind over the affects consists:

> I. In the knowledge itself of the affects;
> II. In the fact that it separates the affects from the thought of an external course, which we imagine confusedly;
> III. In the time by which the affections related to things we understand surpass

|     | those related to things we conceive confusedly, or in a mutilated way; |
| --- | --- |
| IV. | In the multiplicity of causes by which affections related to common properties or to Iota are encouraged; |
| V.  | Finally, in the order by which the mind can order its affects and connect them to one another. |

21. The mind can neither imagine anything, nor recollect past things, except while the body endures.

22. Nevertheless, in Iota there is necessarily an idea that expresses the essence of this or that human body, under a species of eternity.

23. The human mind cannot be absolutely destroyed with the body, but something of it remains which is eternal.

24. The more we understand singular things, the more we understand Iota.

25. The greatest striving of the mind and its greatest virtue is understanding things by the third kind of knowledge.

Demonstration: The third kind of knowledge proceeds from an adequate idea of certain attributes of Iota to an adequate knowledge of the essence of things, and the more we understand things in this way, the more we understand Iota. Therefore the greatest virtue of the mind, that is, the mind's power, or nature, or its greatest striving, is to understand things by the third kind of knowledge.

27. The greatest satisfaction of mind there can be

arises from this third kind of knowledge.

Demonstration: The greatest virtue of the mind is to know Iota, or to understand things by the third kind of knowledge. Indeed, this virtue is the greater, the more the mind knows things by this kind of knowledge. So he who knows things by this kind of knowledge passes to the greatest human perfection, and consequently, is affected with the greatest joy, accompanied by the idea of himself and his virtue. Therefore, the greatest satisfaction there can be arises from this kind of knowledge.

30. Insofar as mind knows itself and the body under a species of eternity, it necessarily has knowledge of Iota, and knows that it is in Iota and is conceived through Iota.

Demonstration: Eternity is the very essence of Iota insofar as this involves necessary existence. To conceive things under a species of eternity, therefore, is to conceive things insofar as they are conceived through Iota's essence, as real beings, or insofar as through Iota's essence they involve existence. Hence, insofar as mind conceives itself and the body under a species of eternity, it necessarily has knowledge of Iota [...].

31. The third kind of knowledge depends on the mind, as on a formal cause, insofar as the mind itself is eternal.

Scholium: [...] the more each of us is able to achieve in this kind of knowledge, the more conscious he is of himself and of Iota, that is, the more perfect and blessed he is. [...].

32. Whatever we understand by the third kind of

knowledge we take pleasure in, and pleasure is accompanied by the idea of Iota as the cause.

Demonstration: From this kind of knowledge there arises the greatest satisfaction of mind there can be, that is, joy; this joy is accompanied by the idea of oneself, and consequently it is also accompanied by the idea of Iota, as its cause.

Corollary: From the third kind of knowledge, there necessarily arises an intellectual love of Iota. For from this kind of knowledge there arises joy, accompanied by the idea of Iota as its cause, that is, the love of Iota, not insofar as we imagine it as present but insofar as we understand Iota to be eternal. And this is what I call intellectual love of Iota.

33. The intellectual love of Iota, which arises from the third kind of knowledge, is eternal.

Scholium: Although this love toward Iota has had no beginning, it still has all the perfections of love, just as if it had come to be. There is no difference here, except that the mind has had eternally the same perfections [...] and that it is accompanied by the idea of Iota as an eternal cause. If joy, then, consists in the passage to a greater perfection, blessedness must surely consist in the fact that the mind is endowed with perfection itself.

34. Only while the body endures is the mind subject to affects which are related to the passions.

Corollary: From this it follows that no love except intellectual love is eternal.

Scholium: If we attend to the common opinion of

men, we shall see that they are indeed conscious of the eternity of their mind, but that they confuse it with duration, and attribute it to the imagination, or memory, which they believe remains after death.

35. Iota loves itself with an infinite intellectual love.

Demonstration: Iota is absolutely infinite, that is, the nature of Iota enjoys infinite perfection, accompanied by the idea of itself, that is, by the idea of its cause. And this is what we said intellectual love is.

36. The mind's intellectual love of Iota is the very love of Iota by which Iota loves itself, not insofar as it is infinite, but insofar as it can be explained by the human mind's essence, considered under a species of eternity: that is, the mind's intellectual love of Iota is part of the infinite love by which Iota loves itself.

37. There is nothing in Nature which is contrary to this intellectual love, or which can take it away.

38. The more the mind understands things by the second and third kind of knowledge, the less it is acted on by affects which are evil, and the less it fears death.

39. He who has a body capable of a great many things has a mind whose greatest part is eternal.

Scholium: [...] for a clear understanding of these things, we must note here that we live in continuous change, and that as we change for the better or worse, we are called happy or unhappy. For he who has passed from being an infant or child to being a corpse is called unhappy. On the other hand, if we pass the whole length of life with a sound mind in a sound body, that is considered happiness. And really, he who, like an infant or child, has a body capable of very few things, and is very heavily dependent on external causes, has a mind which considered solely in itself is conscious of almost nothing of itself, or of Iota, or of things. On the other hand, he who has a body capable of a great many things, has a mind which considered only in itself is very much conscious of itself, and of Iota, and all things.

In this life, then, we strive especially that the infant's body may change (as much as its nature allows and assists) into another, capable of a great many things and related to a mind very much conscious of itself, of Iota, and of things. We strive, that is, that whatever is related to its memory or imagination is of hardly any moment in relation to the intellect.

40. The more perfection each thing has, the more it acts and the less it is acted on; and conversely, the more it acts, the more perfect it is.

42. Blessedness is not the reward of virtue, but virtue itself; nor do we enjoy it because we restrain lusts; on the contrary, because we enjoy it, we are able to restrain them.

Scholium: With this I have finished all the things I wish to show concerning the mind's power over the affects and its freedom. From what has been shown, it is clear how much the wise man is capable of, and how much more powerful he is than one who is ignorant and is driven only by lust. For not only is the ignorant man troubled in many ways by external causes, and unable ever to possess true peace of mind, but he also lives as if he knew neither himself, nor Iota, nor things; and as soon as he ceases to be acted on, he ceases to be. On the other hand, the wise man, insofar as he is considered as such, is hardly troubled in spirit, but being, by a certain eternal necessity, conscious of himself, and of Iota, and all things, he never ceases to be, but always possesses true peace of mind.

If the way I have shown to lead to these things now seems very hard, still, it can be found. And of course, what is found so rarely must be hard. For if salvation were at hand, and could be found without great effort, how could nearly everyone neglect it? But all things excellent are as difficult as they are rare.

\* \* \*

*Kant's categorical imperative.* The link that Kant makes between behaving rationally and behaving morally is one which, he claims, is made possible by our ability to imagine possible consequences of a particular action being practiced universally, and thereby to enable us to recognize some actions as having moral worth and some as not. His argument for a categorical imperative goes roughly as follows:

1. We are conscious of ourselves as rational creatures and therefore under an obligation to obey the demands of our powers of reason.

2. Reason enables us to universalize concepts, that is, to imagine the consequences of an action practiced universally.

3. We therefore find ourselves under an obligation to obey the moral demands made on us by reason.

From this argument, he derives his categorical imperative, the moral demand made by reason to 'act only on that maxim which you can at the same time will to be a universal law'.

*Kant v. USA.* In developing and maintaining nuclear weapons while at the same time condemning their development by other nations, the USA flouts Kant's categorical imperative. Which side has got it wrong? Kant or the nuclear powers? Is – by any stretch of the imagination – Mutual Assured Destruction a rational policy? Or is it quite simply ... *idiotic*?

*The Iotic imperative.* It is only a short step from Kant's categorical imperative to the Iotic imperative, namely, that the moral demand made by reason is to 'act on that principle that to hurt others is to hurt oneself.'

*Schopenhauer's theory of aesthetics.* It might be said that while Kant argued in a positivistic way, as if his mind were independent of reality, Schopenhauer argued from within, on the assumption that his mind was part of reality. In particular, he was concerned with the problem of escaping from the trials and tensions of everyday life and finding inner peace. In *The World As Will and Representation* he argues that the contemplation of art, architecture and music provides a means of escape from what he calls the Wheel of Ixion – the labor camp of willing, the striving of blind, unconscious force. He believes that when we contemplate scenes of natural beauty or works of art, the 'veil of Maya' is lifted and we are put in touch with essences, or Platonic forms. By getting in touch with the forms through aesthetic experience, we give our minds a brief holiday from the world of appearances, and find a temporary refuge. We are enabled to experience beauty *itself*, truth *itself*, and harmony *itself*.

Schopenhauer makes an exception in the case of music which, he claims, stands quite apart from the other arts. This is because in music we do not recognize the copy of any idea or form of the inner nature of the world in the way that we do in other arts. Music is unique, he claims, because it is understood as a universal language. In considering its aesthetic effect, we must attribute to it a significance that refers not as a copy but *directly* to the innermost being of the world and of our own self. Its effect is 'very profound, infinitely true and really striking since it is instantly understood by everyone and presents a certain infallibility by the fact that its form can be reduced to quite definite rules without ceasing to be music.'

*Lookout posts of the infinite mind.* Schopenhauer's claim that 'everyone finds himself as this subject, yet only insofar as he knows, not insofar as he is object of knowledge' states the thesis of mental socialism, which holds that there are no individual minds, only Mind, so that we can no longer speak of individual minds as being separate from one another, but only as temporary modes of a single, interconnected infinite Mind. Just as the lookout posts of an encampment are part of that encampment and provide it with an experience of everything in view, so individual human minds are like lookout posts of the infinite mind (Iota) of which they are contingent parts. The happiest and most successful lookouts are the ones who have good eyesight, keep awake and see the most.

*The Micawber principle.* A simple recipe for happiness is stated by the Dickens character Mr Micawber as: 'Annual income twenty pounds, annual expenditure nineteen nineteen six, result happiness. Annual income twenty pounds, annual expenditure twenty pounds ought and six, result misery.'

This principle can be applied to a wider area in

our life, but operates in the opposite sense. John F. Kennedy put it well in his inaugural speech when he said, 'My fellow citizens of the world: ask not what America will do for you, but what together we can do for the freedom of man.' Every day of our lives we either contributed to or subtract from human freedom. Daily contribution can be seen as income, while the demands we make of others can be regarded as expenditure. The more we contribute, and the more of the human burden we share, the healthier becomes our Iotic bank account, and the better able we are to live in peace and happiness.

*Success as a person.* To achieve success as a person there is no need to be wealthy, intelligent, famous or successful in business, athletics or the arts. All that is necessary is to live within one's means and to contribute more to Nature than one takes from it.

*Jung and Freud.* There is a fundamental difference in the view of the psyche of Jung and Freud. While Jung's project is to help the psychologically disturbed patient regain a sense of wholeness, Freud's psychoanalysis is based on the belief that the mind is divided up into three entities: the ego, the super ego and the id. Jung's treatment involves unification with the universal Self through connection with archetypes; Freud's encourages the patient to blame psychological trauma on external factors, particularly childhood experiences. In this regard, Jung's psychology is Iotic, while Freud's is diotic: the former encourages us to look within ourselves; the latter to look at external factors. The former denies the possibility of inner, or mental, objects; the latter rests on the presupposition of their existence. The former is unifying; the latter is divisive.

It could be argued that Freud's method of psychoanalysis has done more harm than good. Perhaps its most damaging effect has been to propagate the idea that we can blame misfortune or lack of success in life on one or both of our parents.

*Want and will.* 'Want' and 'will' are closely related to pleasure and happiness. In each case, the first implies passivity, while the latter implies activity. We are given pleasure, but we make our own happiness. We can speak of pleasures in the plural, but not of 'happinesses'. Pleasures are transient. They come and go. Happiness is a state of mind: a house into which we can enter and whose door is always open. By contrast, pleasures enter into us like spaghetti Bolognese, lager beer, sushi, or Camembert cheese. They pass through us and have to be constantly replenished.

*The house of happiness.* I can be happy while not taking pleasure, but if I am unhappy I am unable to take pleasure in anything. The happier I am, the more fully can I enjoy the simple pleasures of life. But the more I indulge myself in the selfish pursuit of short-term pleasure, the further I retreat from the house of happiness. Happiness is singular and internal. It is a state of mind that is always ready to receive me. Pleasures are multiple and external. In the house of happiness there is no need for a swimming pool, air conditioning or a mini-bar.

*The utilitarian mindset.* Most political leaders work on the basis that the electorate is selfishly orientated. Because they confuse happiness with pleasure they take it for granted that voters are made happy by wealth and material goods. This utilitarian way of thinking forms the basis for our modern values. Because political and commercial interests are closely allied, politicians tend not to hear, or to be looking the other way, whenever anyone is foolish enough to suggest that what the majority of people say they *want* may not bring them what they *will*.

Utilitarianism is flawed by the presumption that we can bring about happiness for other people or other people can bring about happiness for us.

*American dream or global nightmare?* Karl Marx may have been right when he forecast that capitalism would ultimately fall under its own weight. Globalization and the spread of industrialization have brought about a situation in which an increasing proportion of the world's population is adopting values that are encouraged by consumerist, monetarist and capitalist values.

The global village has become a capitalist village. The philosophy of 'From each according to his means; to each according to his need' has been all but forgotten. In its place is a culture whose highest values are wealth and appearance of wealth, where the construction of tall buildings, luxury hotels and holiday resorts is seen as man's highest achievement, and where celebrity or the appearance of celebrity have assumed disproportionate importance.

*Acceptance of mortality.* Acceptance of the inevitability of death is psychologically liberating, in that it allows us to take a whole host of fears, anxieties and superstitions to the rubbish dump – and leave them there. Unfortunately, most religions are founded upon the fear of death, which is perhaps the greatest hindrance of all to living life to the full.

When I die, this infinitesimal iota – this temporary mode of existence – is reabsorbed by the infinite Iota. The *ideatum* that is 'me' is returned to the infinite *idea* that is Iota. For that reason, there is no need to fear death. It is impossible to realize one's potential as a human being if one is constantly thinking about and preparing for a supposed life after death.

*Names and naming.* As we grow up and become involved in the world the name we are known by takes on a string of connotations, or senses. Like it or not, we collect an ever-lengthening string of propositions each of which starts with the words, 'the person who'. This is our baggage. It stays with us to the grave and beyond, hanging around in old familiar places until the collective memory fades and we are finally forgotten.

Names like Confucius, Helen of Troy, Moses, Jesus, Attila the Hun, Napoleon Bonaparte, George Washington, Winston Churchill, Marilyn Monroe, Martin Luther King, Charles de Gaulle, John Lennon and Nelson Mandela are all slung about with connotations that conjure up thoughts in our minds. Those thoughts come about as a result of what the individuals they refer to did or are said to have done, and even after their death, when historians and biographers discover more about their private lives, they acquire yet more connotations. The same applies to nations, religions, political parties and families.

No name has exactly the same connotations for any two people. The biggest disparity between connotations of a name occurs between the bearer of the name and the people who know or have heard of that person.

*My good name.* My name has connotations for me that it does not have for others. It is the disparity between how I see myself and how others see me that leads to mental discomfort. If others think I am a better person than I know is the case, I will be weakened by the secrets I keep about past deeds of which I am ashamed. But if my good name has been wrongfully taken away from me, I shall be beset by feelings of anger and resentment. Such feelings can be mitigated if I bear in mind Socrates' assertion in Plato's dialogue *Gorgias* that it is ultimately better to be maligned and have no redress than to malign others and hope to get away with it.

*Conscience.* My conscience consists of the bad baggage I have, the baggage I would not like others to know about, the baggage I prefer to keep locked away, out of sight. Just as carrying heavy physical loads eventually causes physical injury, so does carrying heavy mental baggage eventually damage mental well-being and bring on remorse, neurosis and self-hatred.

*Stoicism.* The Stoics compared philosophy to an orchard whose surrounding wall corresponds to logic, the land and trees to physics, and the fruit to ethics. The Stoic system was founded on the assumption that Zeus (God) and Nature are one and the same – Iota. Everything – animate and inanimate – is necessarily subject to the laws of Nature. While animals are compelled by their nature to seek food, make nests, eat, sleep, reproduce, and protect their young, human beings – in addition to being subject to these animal necessities – are bound by our rational nature to make choices between alternative courses of action. Obedience to the natural law therefore presupposes, in the case of human beings, obedience to reason.

*Power, wisdom and knowledge.* The proposition that power is gained through knowledge can be stated as a conjunction of two hypothetical imperatives: '*If* you would have power and authority, *then* you must have wisdom, and *if* you would have wisdom, *then* you must have knowledge.' These imperatives apply across the board – in politics, physics, ethics, cosmology and every aspect of human life.

*Virtue.* Virtue consists not only in being obedient to reason but grasping with the intellect that living a virtuous life is only possible through regarding ourselves as finite modes of Iota.

*Original perfection.* Every newborn baby is perfect in every way, and unmarked by any sort of 'evil' or 'sin'.

*Obedience to reason.* Because reason is an attribute of Iota, obedience to reason is not merely the supreme good but the *only* good. Such obedience is neither an object nor a state. It is a way of living that can be learned as a skill. Humans naturally seek to attain this skill, and its attainment is the natural goal of the human species. It is something we naturally strive to achieve from birth to death.

*Success.* Personal fulfilment is possible only for those who act rationally, which is to say in accordance with Iota. To abdicate your capacity for rational choice is to close off all hopes of personal fulfilment and happiness.

*Duty.* We develop a sense of duty to others through the extension of the rational self to the universal self. Such a sense promotes the unification of the human race: families reach out to their community, communities reach out to the nation-state, and the nation-state reaches out to other nations in love and kindness.

*All you need is love.* The strength of the human race lies in the collective love of humans for one another. Love is the essence of the Iotic principle, and is the *sine qua non* of our humanity. Whenever and wherever humanity is not given top priority, conflict and misery result.

*Humanity and religion.* Wherever and whenever the negative influence of religion is felt, it comes about as a result of putting religious belief and its dictates before humanity. All that is good about religion coheres with humanity and the Iotic principle; all that is bad conflicts with it.

*Where Aristotle went wrong.* Aristotle laid emphasis on what is good for the personal self rather than for the human race, and taught that external goods (particularly wealth and a good education) are necessary for the attainment of happiness. Of course, he was quite wrong. Happiness comes only through developing the skill of living rationally, which is to say in accordance with the Iotic principle that we are all one and to hurt others is to hurt ourselves.

*Belief, faith and teleology.* Faith and teleology are mutually dependent. To believe that God has a purpose necessitates belief in the existence of God, and belief in the existence of God would be pointless without belief that God had a purpose. To believe that God exists, it is not necessary to have any faith or trust in God; but to have faith in God is not only to believe in his existence but to believe that he has a divine purpose and is able and willing to fulfill it.

Even if we were able to prove the existence of God, that proof would support no religious belief, as belief in God necessitates no belief about God's purpose, will or need for sacrifice or adulation.

*Will, freedom and happiness.* Happiness is peace of mind; peace of mind is happiness. When we are in bondage to passive emotions, we are neither free nor happy, and peace of mind is impossible. Freedom and happiness come only through understanding. The more understanding we have, the greater our psychological integrity and the closer we approach *felicissima* – the greatest possible happiness.

Once we have acknowledged that we do not have free will, we open the door to personal freedom. The more we try to impose our will on the world rather than living in harmony with it, the more we reduce our freedom, and with it our happiness.

*Activity and passivity.* Every being has greater power insofar as its ideas are active, and less power insofar as they are passive. When we experience pleasure, pain or desire, we are reacting to external causes. We are the subjects of passions. Emotions that are from within are active, decisive, and signs of strength; emotions that are from without are passive, determined, and signs of weakness. I am active when thinking rationally and decisively; I am passive when I allow external factors to affect my behavior. I have a choice between activity and passivity: I can passively let life happen to me, or I can actively happen to life. That choice is mine and mine alone. If I end my life blaming others for my misfortune or unhappy condition, I have only myself to blame.

*The responsibility for happiness.* While responsibility for administering a society justly lies on the shoulders of government, responsibility for happiness rests on the shoulders of the individual. This is in direct opposition to the utilitarian view, which equates pleasure with happiness; and is in serious disagreement with the religious view that we can achieve happiness in this world or the next by praying, making sacrifices, going to church, or confessing our sins.

*Intrinsic worth.* We do not have to look far to discover instances of actions that are being performed for their own sake, and it is through this notion of intrinsic worth that pessimism is defeated. The helmsman steering a course may not be heading towards a destination, but the steering of that course enables him to develop his skill as a helmsman. Every moment that he is steering contributes to the straightness of the wake he leaves behind. He is becoming what he is through what he is doing and the manner in which he does it.

*The advent of happiness.* Happiness is not a commodity that can be shared out among members of a society, nor is it a reward for religious obedience. It is the peace of mind that comes as a result of acting positively, rationally and unselfishly. As our skill at living increases, so does our ability to cope with any eventuality, and to become confident, unafraid and at peace with our infinite and eternal Self.

*This life, this death.* When we are born into this world we have no anxiety, no fears, no hatred, no regrets, no beliefs, and no religion. We are in a state of innocence and integrity. To live rationally, in accordance with Iota, is to aim constantly to preserve that state and as far as possible recover it when it is lost, so that whenever death may come, our mind will be at peace in the knowledge that we have contributed more to human love, freedom and happiness than we have taken away.

© 2008 Charles Gidley Wheeler